GRAMPIAN CURIOSITIES

Robert Smith

First published in 2005 by
Birlinn Ltd
West Newington House
10 Newington Road
Edinburgh EH9 1QS

www.birlinn.co.uk

ISBN10: 1 84158 397 9
ISBN13: 978 184158 397 6

British Library Cataloguing-in-Publication Data
A catalogue record for this book is available from the British Library

Typeset by Andrew Sutterby
Printed and bound by GraphyCems, Spain

CONTENTS

ACKNOWLEDGEMENTS

When I wrote *Aberdeen Curiosities* a few years ago, I described
it as being about 'odd people and strange happenings' and, like
Alice in Wonderland, it got 'curioser and curioser'. This new
book, covering a wider area in Aberdeen and the North-east,
offers even more curious tales.

Of course, none of it would have come to light if it hadn't
been for the great many people who once again helped to open
up this wonderland. They have my grateful thanks.

Robert Smith
Aberdeen, July 2005

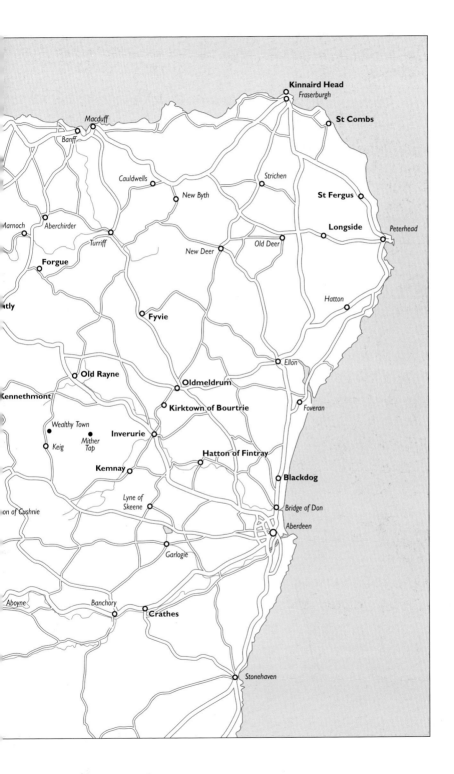

1

WOW OF RIVVEN

'The Road to the Kirk o' Rivven
Faur gangs mair dead nor livin.'

Wow! here is a curiosity to make you think. To find it you have to follow the road to Rivven, which breaks away from the Huntly–Keith road and pushes north by Cairnie to the windy acres between the Balloch Hill and the Bin. In this remote corner of the north-east, the village of Rivven slumbers in the shadow of the Balloch. Its name has always intrigued me, as has that bleak little couplet about the dead and living (see above).

Nobody knows when it was written, but it must have been a long time ago for the kirk has been a ruin for centuries. All that remains of it is a single wall, curiously crow-stepped only on one side, with a massive belfry. Inside the belfry is an ancient bell called the Wow of Rivven. Behind that bell lies a curious story, stranger even than the 'dead nor livin' verse.

This gaunt ruin is all that is left of the Kirk o' Rivven.
The bell still hangs in the belfry, but nobody pulls the
chain that hangs from it.

Before hearing about the Wow of Rivven I had been reading a book called *Raw Spirit,* written by the Scottish author Iain Banks. It was about tasting whisky in the Highlands and in it was a passage which said he had been driving to Machrie, a hotel on the island of Islay, when he saw a buzzard.

'Oh, wow,' he cried. 'A buzzard! Look!'

Toby, the author's friend, wasn't impressed. 'Ha!' he said bitterly, glaring at the thing. 'Buzzards. They're the reason we don't have any songbirds in Ballivicar.'

It wasn't buzzards and songbirds that were in my mind when I read these lines. It was the author's curious reaction, his use of a word that has been creeping into the English language for some time – 'wow!' Everybody seems to be at it. Where did it spring from? Why did it spread like some comic's catch-phrase? It was while I was pondering on this that I heard about the mysterious 'wow' in the old kirk yard at Rivven and decided to see it for myself.

So I took the road to Rivven, a road I had never been on, to a village I had never seen. I knew nothing about Rivven except that it was a nickname. The real name was Ruthven, which came from *rath bheinne,* a hill fort. I knew, too, that it was a common name in north-east counties, that in Banffshire it was Rathven and in older writings it was Rothven. I also learned that there was a Ruthven in Logie Coldstone and that it was on the slope of a hill which had definite remains of a hill fort on its top. The church dated back to the early thirteenth century and had no regular minister preaching there later than 1630, although the minister at nearby Botary took services.

In the tree-shrouded kirk yard there was a stone near the belfry that stood out from the rest. This is what it said

ERECTED
By the inhabitants of Huntly
In memory of
JOHN McBEY
Better known by the name of
'Feel Jock' or 'the Colonel',
he died there the 15 March 1848
Aged about 71 years.
His remains rest here at his
own express request near his

> special favourite the Bell of
> Ruthven. or as he was wont to
> call it 'the Wow' the double
> peals of which he imagined
> to signify 'come hame, come
> hame.'

John McBey was a foundling, abandoned in a moss near Huntly and brought up on the parish. A Huntly woman, Mrs Alexander Ogg, took him under her wing and he looked on her as his mother. When she died she was buried at the Kirk of Ruthven and it was there that Feel Jock first heard the Bell of Rivven sounding out its double peal. He thought it seemed to say 'Come hame, come hame,' and when Mrs Ogg was buried he thought the bell was mourning her – 'She wowed sair for my mither,' he said.

How Feel Jock came to speak of the bell as the Wow nobody knows. When he first heard its peal ringing dolefully over the kirk yard he was transfixed, and it may be that the cry came out instinctively. He would often squint up at the bell and cry 'Dae ye ken me, Wow? Dae ye like me? I like you.' The local boys would torment him, hiding among the gravestones and shouting 'The Wow disnae like ye, Jock.'

Some folk might have laughed at Feel Jock's belief in the Wow, but it seemed as if the old bell had cast its spell over the villagers as well. It is said that when the bell tolled for funerals they could tell from its tone if someone was being called. 'The bell's sorry today. There'll be another funeral,' they would say.

The Napoleonic Wars were in the news then and Feel Jock, hearing the talk about it, got one of his benefactors to rig him up in military 'uniform' – a coat and trousers of a dark grey cloth and a yellow collar and yellow narrow cuffs. He strutted about Rivven in all his glory, and his greatest pride was the badge on his arm – a piece of cloth cut out in the shape of a bell with its tongue hanging out of its mouth. He liked people to call him 'colonel'.

The folk of Rivven were as proud of their bell as Jock, conscious of its beautiful tone and its historic links. It was said to have been brought over from the Netherlands. It had the date 1643 stamped on it and a Latin inscription meaning 'Every kingdom divided against itself will fall to pieces.' If the people in the neighbouring village of Cairnie had been given their way, Ruthven *might* have fallen to pieces, for at the beginning of the nineteenth century Cairnie, looking for a bell for a new church they had built, cast envious eyes on the bell at Ruthven, whose kirk had been a ruin since 1721.

The villagers of Cairnie petitioned the Duke of Gordon for permission to take the bell for their new kirk. He gave the go-ahead provided the Ruthven folk were in agreement. The Rivvenites were totally opposed to the idea and John Wilson, a brogue maker, rung the Wow to call the people together in its defence.

A party from Cairnie, headed by the schoolmaster, set off with a horse and cart to take away the bell. They were met by a host of Rivven folk, men and women, armed with all kinds of implements, the women with aprons full of stones. The leader of the Cairnie invaders told them they had a letter from the Duke of Gordon authorising the removal of the bell. The defenders insisted that the letter be read and when it was a great cheer went up for it contained the statement that the Ruthven people had to give their agreement.

The schoolmaster and his people were driven off, their cart smashed to pieces, and the bell was taken down and put under lock and key in the Mill of Ruthven to prevent a midnight attempt on it. That was the end of the Battle of the Wow.

Some say that the Cairnie people made a second attempt to get the bell at another time, and that 'they succeeded in taking it down and carrying it as far as Drummyduan, on the farm of Auchanachie, about a mile from Ruthven'. The bell, however, became so supernaturally heavy that ten men were unable to move it from the ground, yet two men managed to carry it back to Ruthven!

I wanted to go and see the Wow, maybe even to hear it ringing. So I headed up the Huntly–Keith road, stopping at a petrol station to ask the way. Iain Anderson, who runs the petrol station, pointed across the fields to a row of houses and said 'That's Cairnie.' He told me he was born and bred there, and he knew all about Rivven and its Wow. He said a wee hump-backed brig as you go into Cairnie was the bridge where the Rivven men caught up with the Cairnie men who had stolen the Wow. They got their bell back, and pitched the cart into the burn.

I asked Iain if the bell was ever rung. He laughed and said they used to ring it at the New Year when they'd a few drams. There was no rope then and they climbed up the belfry, but the stonework was uncertain and the wood wasn't very good. They didn't actually ring the bell in case it broke away and fell to the ground, but they took hold of the tongue and rapped it. Feel Jock had heard the bell ringing and was stunned by the sound, but to Iain and other people who heard it there was nothing special about it.

I left Carnie and went on my way. I was on the road to the Kirk o' Rivven, 'faur gangs mair dead nor livin', but I'm not sure that holds good today. I passed Auchanachie, where the Wow was taken in Cairnie's second raid. The House of Auchanachie was a sixteenth-century tower house and is now a farmhouse.

The first person I met in Ruthven was Bob Green, who lives in a big white house that was once the post office. He came from Lancashire and has been there for three years. He showed me a photograph of his house when it was thatched and acted as the village shop as well as the post office. It wasn't the only thing that had changed in Rivven. It was hard to believe that this back o' beyond community had a two-teacher school with eighty pupils, that the mill wheel whirled round to produce the grain, that horses lined up at the smiddy to be shod and that the village once held a regular market. There is a market cross there to prove it.

Bob said that people came from all over the country, and even from abroad, to see the Wow of Rivven. He took me to the gate of the kirk yard, where he pointed out a curiously shaped stone embedded in the wall near the gate. This was an effigy, dating from the early fifteenth century, of Thomas Gordon of Daugh, better known as Tam o' Rivven, who fought a battle with the Abbot of Grange on the slopes of the Balloch Hill. The abbot was killed on the spot and Tam was also mortally wounded and died a short distance from the scene of the fight. He is buried in the Ruthven churchyard. A ballad had this to say about Tam, 'Peal'd from the church of Ruthven's bell! The doleful sound of parting knell, There you may see in passing by Bold Tam, in sculptured effigy.'

Tam was represented as a knight in full armour, with the visor of his helmet raised. There was originally an inscription in the sword belt around his body. Sadly, long exposure has erased all the markings. Bob left me there to salute the famous Tam and to pay my respects to the Wow. It was quiet and peaceful in the kirk yard, cut off from the outside world, the ancient tombstones around me holding their secrets.

I made my way to where the remains of the church stood darkly against the wall. The massive belfry rose defiantly above me, towering over the rows of tombstones in the old kirk yard and guarding a bell that was nearly four centuries old. The sun was shining, casting a shadow on it, and the branch of a tree waved gently in front of it, as if protecting the Wow. I could see the bell hanging there, big and black. It was still and silent now and I wished it could ring out so that I could hear its compelling sound and understand why so many people had fallen under its spell. There was a chain hanging from it and I was told that it had been rung, but I avoided the temptation – the Wow might not have liked it! I was thinking of poor, half-witted Feel Jock standing where I was standing, looking up at the Wow and asking it if it liked him. 'Dae ye like me, Wow? I like you.' I could hear, too, that plaintive call, 'Come hame, come hame,' as if the Wow was beckoning people to a better place.

The belfry on the ruined Kirk o' Rivven.

I left Ruthven reluctantly. That small, tidy kirk yard seemed to me still to belong to the past, and up in that gloomy belfry is the only link with the Wow of Rivven and its curious story. Some time after my visit I came across an article, 'The Wow of Rivven', by George MacDonald, the Huntly author, who wrote fairy tales and fantasy novels. He was born in 1804 and died in 1905, so he lived through the time of Ruthven's fairy tale.

According to MacDonald, a woman called Ella Scott was Feel Jock's benefactor. Ella was a little girl when she first met him. 'She looked at him with some terror on his uncouth appearance, and with much wonderment on his strange dress. This wonder was heightened by a conversation she overheard one day in the street, between the fool and a little pale-faced boy, who approaching him respectfully, said 'Weel, Cornel!' 'Weel, laddie!' was the reply. 'Fat dis the Wow say, Cornel?' 'Come hame, come hame!' answered the colonel.

There was no mention of Mrs Ogg in MacDonald's story. Ella Scott was at his side when he died. 'Hearing that he was ill, Ella ventured one bright spring day to go to see him. When she entered the miserable room where he lay, he held out his hand to her with something like a smile and muttered feebly and painfully "I'm ga'in' to the Wow, nae to come back again." Ella could not restrain her tears, while the old man, looking fixedly at her, though with meaningless eyes, muttered for the last time "Come hame, come hame!"'

2

WATTY, TOWN DRUMMER

It was four o'clock in the morning and Watty Leith was beginning his long walk through the empty streets of Aberdeen. He wore a 'lum' hat on his head and sported a flamboyant waistcoat and a big bow tie. A heavy side-drum hung around his neck, reaching down to his ankles. The two drumsticks in his hands began to beat a steady tattoo as he went on his way . . .

Walter Leith was Aberdeen's town drummer, the knocker-up who got people out of their beds before the crack of dawn so that, as his employers said, 'laborious folks may pass to their labours in due and convenient time'. The first time I saw Watty was in a picture entitled 'Seaton's View of Castle Street, 1806.' John Ewen, a local jeweller and councillor, had employed Mr R. Seaton, a self-styled 'landscape painter and drawing master', to execute two sets of drawings – one in colour, the other in Indian ink – as 'Views of New and Old Aberdeen'. Prints and engravings of them were sent to subscribers.

Seaton was said to 'paint portraits of gentlemen's favourite horses and dogs and other animals', and his success in his first tilt at the art market in Aberdeen encouraged him to undertake another of John Ewen's 'views'. In January 1807 an advertisement announced the completion of his 'View of Castle Street of Aberdeen on a Market Day, in which Portraits of some well-known Characters in Aberdeen are introduced.' It was to be disposed of by way of a lottery.

The Castlegate in those days was used as a promenade by all sorts of people: bankers and provosts, washerwomen and beggars, chapmen and strutting recruiting sergeants, fiddlers and fishwives, drunks and vendors. Here, they caught up on the town gossip, hawked the latest almanacs, played the fiddle, sang and sold meat pies, and tempted people with 'dainties'. There was no dearth of characters for Mr Seaton's 'View of Castle Street'.

The fishwives sold their goods on the steps of the Plainstanes – 'real finans and partans at three ha'pence a pair all so sweetly fresh'. Seaton's sketch showed John Milne, the town's hangman, claiming a fish from the basket of one of the fishwives. It was part of the hangman's 'perks'.

John Ewen himself was there, a tall man talking to two ladies, and near him was the Rev. Alexander Alcock, minister of St Paul's Episcopal Chapel, although some expressed doubts about the likeness of the last two 'alleged portraits'. Beside the Tolbooth steps a 'leerie' was seen talking to someone, holding a long lamp-lighter in his hand. Watty, the town drummer, was on the right-hand side of the picture, in front of three fishwives displaying their wares.

Waking up drowsy Aberdonians was done in different ways over the years. The city fathers liked to bring in a variety of musical instruments to avoid people becoming accustomed to the wake-up sound. One of the earliest instruments was a hand bell. Burgh records mention the duties of the bellman, who had to be out of bed between three and four o'clock in the morning to take up his duties. He had to call the townsfolk to the Market Cross to witness the sale of a house or a piece of land in any part of the town. He had to announce when fish were for sale at the Fish Cross, or when special religious services were to be held in the town's church. He even had to call out the city's sixteenth-century 'Dad's Army' – male members of the community between the ages of sixteen and sixty – who had to buckle on their armour and weapons of war, and assemble at the Castlegate, ready to go forth at any hour of the day or night to defend their city.

The hand bell gave way to the curiously named swesch. It may have sounded like a piece of squashed fruit, but in fact it was a kind of trumpet. The first town swesch-man, or swescher, was a John Cowper, who was appointed on 25 August 1566. His duties included playing the swesch in time of war as well as peace, and at sport and play when required.

Cowper, the swesch-man, was switched to the Almany whistle or flute, and was called the town's whistler. Jamieson's *Scottish Dictionary* described the instrument as a flageolet of a very small size, used by children. Whistles of this kind were originally imported from Almanie, Germany. Cowper was instructed 'to pass through the town at four o'clock in the morning, and eight at night, playing upon the Almany whistle, accompanied by a servant playing on the tambourine, whereby craftsmen, their servants and all other laborious folks, warned and excited, would get out of their beds and go to work'.

Cowper also became the town drummer, and claimed two years' salary from the town for banging on the town drum. He got his money, but in 1569 he was made redundant when the council decided to stop playing musical alarm clocks with swesches and flutes. It was decided to ring the parish kirk bell instead.

The bagpipes were also used against sleepyheads. The piper was an official of considerable importance in those days, for not only was he a town's functionary but his was also a government appointment. He received a payment from the lord high treasurer when he was called upon to play the 'pipes when royalty visited the town'. The piper gave them a blaw for the last time in 1630, when the town council decided to dispense with his services. The reason was said to be that visitors to the town had complained about being roused from their slumber at an early hour by the strains of the bagpipes.

So that was 'Seaton's View of Castle Street, 1806'. It was, as had been promised, put up for lottery and in the beginning of February the *Journal* announced that the winning ticket – number 67 – was held by a lady, who had 'carried off the prize of Mr Seaton's beautiful view of Castle Street'. It eventually came into the possession of James Rettie, a local historian, who sold it to the town council to hang in the municipal buildings.

The 1806 picture had its imitators, but there was nothing to match it until an artist called J.W. Allan produced 'Hay's Print of Castle Street, 1840'. John Hay was the publisher. This 'View' had more 'characters' in it, a large number drawn from the city's 'best-known and most respectable citizens'. These 'striking portraits', as they were called, were 'inserted by Mr P. Mackenzie, a young and talented artist in Aberdeen'. Many notable citizens stalked across the Castlegate in Hay's print. There, for instance, was the portly figure of a man rejoicing in the name of Ignatius Massie, who was manager of the Gasworks, and one-time auctioneer, and Provost James Milne, who was nicknamed 'Birdie' but nevertheless once led a charge of police against a rowdy mob. There, too, was Henry Paterson, a 'daring speculator', who was said by rumourmongers to have manured his fields with bank notes, and James Johnston, manager of the Aberdeen Bank, who featured in a poem by James Ramsay, editor of the *Journal*.

> Forth from his mansion, just at ten o'clock,
> Struts the learned Banker, like a turkey cock
> Burly and big, behold him sail along,

Wit in his wink and wisdom in his tongue!
Through Silver Street he steers for Golden Square,
Soon Diamond Street proclaims his presence there
Then Union Street must feel in all its stones
The heavy burden of his beef and bones.
Here – let us mark him as with look profound
And solemn gait he clears the granite ground
Right to the Bank – the scene of all his labour,
Where Willie G— was once his drouthy neighbour:
Famed Greece and Rome may jointly claim his nose,
His cheek is red – the cause you may suppose;
His mouth is but a so-so perforation
Through which to dole the frequent long oration!

That verse by John Ramsay appeared in George Walker's book *Aberdeen Awa'* nearly half a century after Hay's print first appeared. Walker was said to have given the fullest account of the 'best-known and most respectable citizens' depicted in the Print. He wrote about Provost James Hadden, 'old, venerable and, after the storms of life' highly honoured, and about Dr Joseph Robertson, who had 'made his mark and secured a place in the rolls of fame'.

He picked out the 'decidedly distinguished form' of Sir Alexander Bannerman (knighted in 1851), discussing the affairs of the nation with Sir Michael Bruce of Scotston, who, as his senior in rank and dignity, was represented as on horseback. Then there was the 'smart, active, life-like form of John Angus, the town clerk, on his way to his place of business in the town house', and after him 'the full face and form of Councillor William Philip, of broad and free speech notoriety, whose pithy sayings set many tables in a roar and in their laughter-producing results promoted digestion, and thus helped to prolong the lives of many citizens'. Alongside Philip, 'with his hands in his pockets, and looking a very unconcerned spectator', stood John Hay, while next to him walked Sir Alexander Anderson, arm-in-arm with Sir Thomas Blaikie, discussing contemplated city improvements.

Note: George Walker explained why he had gone to the trouble of identifying and describing the figures in Hay's print. 'Hay connects in one view the spiritual agencies and their material results – the creators and their creations – and thus it is invaluable, because it is a work of genius.' The print, he said, was getting increasingly valuable, and a whole generation had passed away, so it was worthwhile giving the names of the people who figured in the picture.

3

GREAT HAIRCUT RIOT

The Great Haircut Riot in 1919 has never featured much, if at all, in our history books. There were, after all, other things to think about at that time, for instance, the First World War was over and food rationing was about to end, German crews scuttled their ships at Scapa Flow, a gunner was accidentally killed at Torry Battery, and Peterhead and Fraserburgh fishermen decided to stop herring fishing until a minimum of thirty shillings per cran was obtained. The Great Haircut Riot, however, was different – a curiosity if you like – for you seldom heard of riots being led by women and backed by a horde of stone-throwing children.

The Aberdeen riot did find a place in one history book. This was a useful little publication entitled *A Record of Events in Aberdeen and the North, 1801–1927* and priced at five shillings. There were two entries about the riot, the first of which was 'Riot of a huge crowd of people in the Gallowgate, Aberdeen, over the cutting of the hair of certain girls in the Middle School, June 16.' The second entry read 'Further demonstrations in Aberdeen against hair cutting in schools, June 17.'

So what lay behind these two brief entries? The news was broken to the public in the *Aberdeen Daily Journal* of 18 June 1919. 'Aberdeen "Haircut" Rioting' said the headlines. 'Demonstrations by Pupils Throughout City.' The readers were told how on 16 June a crowd of several hundred people had gathered outside the Middle School at the Gallowgate. They were mostly 'irate parents', women who resented the fact that some girl pupils had been given a haircut by the medical staff of the Aberdeen education authority. It had nothing to do with hair styles – the problem was 'verminous heads'.

Through the afternoon and on until midnight they waited at the gates of the school under the impression that the medical officer was inside the building. They made 'forceful efforts' to get into the school. Between eight and ten o'clock, according to the *Journal*, the 'situation became ugly'. Stones were thrown and many of the windows of the school were smashed.

When the police arrived on the scene they came in for 'some bad usage', but this was limited to light missiles being thrown at them by the youthful and irresponsible element in the crowd. Repeated rushes were made towards the gateway. The police, almost half a dozen in number under an Inspector Smith, dealt with the situation with the utmost tact and desisted from the use of force. The missile-throwing gradually ceased and about ten o'clock a heavy shower of rain put a different kind of damper on things. Many watchers went home.

Later, the crowd grew again and people going home from a night out in the town saw the disturbance and joined the crowd. Another attempt was made to rush the north entrance, but there were now about thirty policemen on the spot and the throng was easily dispelled.

None of the constables was any worse for the jostling and stone throwing, but a little girl had her head badly cut. Although women predominated in the crowd, the disorderliness came mostly from the juvenile element. Most of the men were content to stay in the background and watch the proceedings, but they were obviously sympathetic to the women and the protest they had taken up.

The police were still hanging about the school at one o'clock in the morning, and the whole affair might have fizzled out a lot earlier if the 'rioters' had been told that the medical officer had left the school in the afternoon.

Two days later the *Journal* told its readers that there had been demonstrations by the pupils of several schools and that the town was 'considerably excited at the disturbance'. Such a state of matters, it said, could not be ignored, and a special meeting of the health committee was held to discuss the matter. The following statement was given out after the meeting.

There is no truth in the rumours that have been prevalent regarding the wholesale cutting of girls' hair.

There has been no alteration in the method adopted and carried out for the last ten years in regard to the cleansing of verminous heads.

It is only as a last resource that a girl's hair is cut, and this after at least two warning notices have been sent to the girl's parents.

Vermin in a child's head is prejudicial to the health of the child itself, and a danger to other children in the same school.

Not more than one or two girls in every thousand have to be treated by haircutting and only 9 per cent of the girls are found to have dirty hair, while in 1910 the percentage was 40. This, in itself, shows that the method adopted by the education authority is effectual.

George Duncan, advocate, chairman of the education authority, visited the scene of the disturbance with Col. Dawson, director of education, and approved the action of the health committee. Other members visited the school later in the day, and general regret was expressed that so much 'wanton destruction' had been done to the windows by stone throwing. 'Almost every window facing the street and the open space of the Gallowgate was smashed or cracked, and as glass is five times its pre-war price the bill will be considerable,' said their report. 'Hundreds of people came from all over the city to see the damage that had been done.'

The *Journal* said that the attitude of parents of girls who had the scissors applied to their hair could be well understood. Their allegation was that the hair cutting was done without previous warning. The school medical authorities claimed to have the power under the Act of 1908 to take steps to clean 'the persons of any children infected with vermin or in a foul condition. They only took the extreme step when warnings had failed to produce any apparent improvement in the condition of a child. It was taken not merely for the sake of the child itself but for the protection of other children.'

That then was the Great Haircut Riot. It appeared at first to be a storm in a teacup – the work of the school went on despite the broken windows – but as more information about the 'riot' emerged it became clear that it was bigger than had been thought. The ripples from the commotion at the Gallowgate spread through the town. Quite a number of primary schools gave support to the protesters by marching to the school, while other pupils, mostly boys, played truant.

'Several crowds gathered,' reported the *Journal*, 'and marched by Broad Street and also by St Paul Street and the Gallowgate to the Middle School, where they engaged in cheering and made a good deal of noise. The leader of one group of girls, most of them apparently over fourteen years of age, carried a miniature Union Jack, and seemed to regard this as her insignia.'

It seemed as if rebellious pupils from half the city schools had come out in support of their shorn sisters' protest, but there were other, more likely, reasons for their actions. The *Journal* reported a demonstration at Skene Square School 'where the scholars seemed inclined to take a holiday at the beach'. There was a good deal of shouting and cheering, though what it was for seemed to be very hazy in the minds of the demonstrators. It was said to be a 'sympathetic strike'.

The target for the strikes was still Dr Rose, the medical officer, who had given the demonstrators the slip on the first day. The marchers thought they were hot on his trail when a nurse was spotted standing beside one of the upstairs windows of Frederick Street School. The crowd of women and children who gathered at the school gates were sure that the 'villain of the piece' was inside. The police assured them that he was not, but nobody believed them because it was argued that if a nurse was there she could be there only to cut off some poor girl's hair. The school janitor was struck by a missile and it looked as if things would get ugly, but it quietened down, although a big crowd still remained in front of the school.

The drama shifted to Dr Rose's residence in Rubislaw Terrace, where there was the usual shouting and waving of flags, but in the end the police moved them on. Meanwhile, there was a series of processions along Union Terrace at different times. One took place at night when a meeting of the primary schools committee was being held. The crowd, largely of boys and girls, booed as it passed the offices of the education authority and 'went on its noisy way'.

It was estimated that there were more than 2,000 people outside the Middle School on 16 June, but after two days the 'strikers' were back at school, no doubt wondering nervously what lay in store for them. The tak'a's [attendance officers] chased up the missing youngsters. The older boys were given the scud [strap), with the severest belting going to those who had to be rounded up from their homes.

Those were the days when there was a great deal of sensitivity about what were called 'the beasties' – vermin in children's hair, which could spread like plague through a school. Friday night wasn't only bath night: it was the night in most working-class homes when bone combs were taken out and heads were examined for any unwanted visitors.

4

THE QUEEN'S DWARF

I first saw Jeffrey Hudson, the smallest man in Britain, standing on a staircase in Fyvie Castle. It was actually a statue I was looking at, for the man himself had been dead for four hundred years. But he was still very impressive – all three and a half feet of him. He was a dwarf, a midget who fought a duel, a tiny man who became a queen's favourite, a Lilliputian adventurer who travelled abroad and was captured by pirates and sold as a slave.

I have seen some interesting curiosities at Fyvie Castle. I have looked up at Fyvie's famous trumpeter blowing his horn, I have heard about the Mill of Tiftie's Annie, I have wondered at the mysterious dripping stone, and I have gazed at Mussel-mou'd Charlie Leslie consorting with the lairds and their ladies in the picture gallery. But I have never heard of a dwarf who could jump out of a hot venison pie.

The statue of Jeffrey Hudson clutching his musket.

To begin at the beginning. Jeffrey Hudson was born in Oakland, Rutland, in England, in 1619. His father was a butcher, who kept bulls for George Villiers, first Duke of Buckingham. Neither of his parents was undersized, but when Jeffrey was seven years old he was only eighteen inches high. When he was thirty he shot up to three feet six inches.

About that time, Charles I and his fifteen-year-old French queen, Henrietta Maria, passed through Rutland. The Duke of Buckingham gave a dinner in their honour and laid on a special treat for his guests – a huge, sumptuous pie. Hudson was brought on to the table concealed in the pie, and when it was opened out he jumped. Some reports say it was a cold pie, which was more likely, for otherwise poor Jeffrey would have been roasted. It was also said that he was singing the 'four and twenty blackbirds' song when he appeared.

When Henrietta saw him emerging from the pie she was 'amused by his sprightly way' and immediately took him into her service. It was a relationship that was to last for fifteen years. They were virtually inseparable.

The earliest account of the queen's dwarf came in a book, *The Worthies of England*, edited by Thomas Fuller, published in 1662. This is what it said,

Dr Fuller hath already placed him in the List of Memorable Persons, tho he knew but little of his Story. It is Jeoffrey Hudson the Dwarf, memorable on several Accounts. He was the Son of one John Hudson, a person of very mean Condition, but of a lusty Stature and so were all his Children, except this Jeoffrey, born in the year 1619. Being above seven years old and scarce eighteen inches in highth, he was taken into the Family of the late Duke of Buckingham at Burly on the Hill, in this County, as a Rarity of Nature, and the Court being about that time in Progress there, he was served up to the Table in a cold Pye. After the Marriage of King Charles the first with the excellent Princess Henrietta Maria of France, he was presented to that Queen, and became her Dwarf.

In 1630 Jeffrey went to France with a party sent to bring back a midwife for the queen's approaching confinement, but the ship was captured by a Flemish pirate and the royal travellers were taken to Dunkirk. They were released after a few days and sent over the border to France. Jeffrey had with him £2,000 in jewels and rich goods given to him by the ladies, but the Dunkirk men took these from him.

This little man was often the butt of cruel jokes about his height, despite the fact that he had been made a captain of horse during the Civil War. There is nothing to show that he took part in any battle, but he was intensely proud of his title. It was this, perhaps, that made him even more sensitive to jibes about his height, and he was determined that he would be treated with respect. He let it be known that the next one to insult him would be challenged to a duel.

To Charles Crofts, son of Sir Henry Crofts of Saxham, Suffolk, this was the greatest joke of all – Little Jeffrey challenging a full-grown man to fight him in a duel. It would be the talk of the town and he would face him with a garden water sprinkler to 'dampen the little fellow's powder'. They fought on horses so that Hudson would be on the same level as Crofts. The result was that the queen's dwarf promptly shot and killed Crofts. He was threatened with imprisonment for it, but the Queen saved him and he had to leave Paris.

There was another curious but dubious story about Hudson in combat with a turkey cock. It was in fact a lampoon, and Sir William Devenant is said to have written this verse about the clash,

Jeffrey straight was thrown, when faint and weak,
The cruel fowl assaults him with his beak,
A lady midwife now he there by chance
Espied, that came along with him from France.

'A heart brought up in war, that ne'er before
This time could bow,' he said, 'doth now implore
Thou, that delivered hast so many, be
So kind of nature as deliver me.'

There is nothing to show if Jeffrey resented this lampoon, but it was said he was 'a consequential personage' and rarely showed bad temper when domestics and courtiers teased him. He apparently, however, had many squabbles with the king's gigantic porter.

In the winter of 1644 he was at sea again and for the second time was attacked by pirates. They were the dreaded Turkish corsairs. The historian James Wright wrote this about it, 'He was a second time taken Prisoner at Sea, but that was a much more fatal activity than the first. It was a Turkish Pirate that took and carried him to Barbary, where he was sold, and remain'd a slave for many years.'

Jeffrey was fifty years old when he returned to England. He lived quietly in the country on a pension subscribed to by the Duke of Buckingham and several others. There were no fine ladies now to fuss around him and give him money and clothing. Little Jeffrey – 'Lord Minimus' as he was nicknamed – was forgotten. He is said to have died alone and in poverty in the 1680s.

Yet the dwarf who charmed a queen lived on in a number of paintings and sculptures by well-known artists. Five paintings were made of him. He was fourteen years old when van Dyck produced 'Queen Henrietta with Sir Jeffrey Hudson' in 1633. Jeffrey was 'knighted' as a joke by the king, and he often used the title. In the painting, the queen, who was a petite lady of twenty-four, seemed much taller beside Jeffrey than she actually was. She wore a satin hunting dress and her hand rested on a monkey sitting on Jeffrey's shoulder. It was his pet, called Pug.

There is an interesting picture of a suit of armour made for John of Gaunt, son of Edward III about 1535, while alongside it is a small armour said to have been made for Jeffrey Hudson. It dated from 1630 and looked like a toy suit of armour for an infant. Thomas Fuller, in *The Worthies of England,* mentioned a curious comment made by Jeffrey about his height.

That which in my opinion seems the most Observable is what I have heard himself several times affirm, that between the 7th Year of his Age and the 30th he never grew any thing considerable, but after thirty he shot up in a little time to that highth of stature which he remain'd at in his old age, viz. about three foot and nine Inches. The cause of this he ascribed (how truly I know not) to the hardship, much labour, and beating, which he endured when a Slave to the Turks. This seems a Paradox, how that which hath been observed to stop the growth of other persons, should be the cause of his. But let the Naturalists reconcile it.

Jeffrey Hudson, the Queen's Dwarf, on guard inside Fyvie Castle.

Whatever his height or weight, women were attracted to him. This tiny midget was said by Thomas Heywood, the dramatist, to be 'one of the prettiest, neatest and well-proportioned small men that ever Nature bred'. Henry Stonecastle, a well-known publisher, said 'The ladies were very fond of him. He could make married men Cuckolds without making them jealous.' This was described by Nick Page, author of *Lord Minimus* (2002), as 'salacious nonsense'.

Nearly four centuries after popping out of that pie, Little Jeffrey still casts a spell over the ladies. Janis Maroney (pronounced Marnie) is a helper at Fyvie Castle. She came to Aberdeen from Norfolk twelve years ago, and has been at the castle for eleven years. It was in the grounds of the castle that she first saw the figure of Jeffrey Hudson, wearing his funny helmet, clutching a musket as big as he was, and looking quite magnificent. She was fascinated by him, and by the story behind him. Now she has a thick folder packed with cuttings on the queen's dwarf, pictures of him and letters from other Jeffrey Hudson addicts. She also has copies of 'Royal Accounts Relating to the Secret Service of Charles II.' There are entries such as the one in 1680 awarding £20 to William Green and Richard Jarvis 'for seizing John Nicholls, a priest', or another awarding £22 16s. 'To Edward Murphy and others, witnesses relating to the popish plot in Ireland, on an allowance of 12s. per week, to the 11th, 13th and 15th of April 1681.' Then there is a brief entry in 1681 'To Dr Oates – £10'. Dr Oates was Titus Oates, the English conspirator who fabricated the 1678 Popish plot, a supposed Catholic conspiracy to kill Charles II, to burn London and massacre Protestants. His perjury brought about the execution of many innocent Catholics. There are two pages of accounts and in the middle of them two entries stand out: 'To Capt Jeffrey Hudson, as of free guift and royal bounty – £50', and in 1681 'To Capt Jeffrey Hudson, as of free guift – £20'. Janis Maroney also had correspondence with Oakham Ales, who now brew a pleasant bitter called Jeffrey Hudson Bitter or JHB. There is little she doesn't know about the wee man with the musket.

How did the queen's dwarf land up in this part of the world? Well, when Alexander Forbes Leith was the laird of Fyvie, he bought Little Jeffrey at an auction in England for ten pounds. He no doubt bought him because as a child Charles I often stayed at Fyvie Castle, but he probably never knew that he had an incredible bargain. In 1984, the National Trust took over Nostell Priory, near Wakefield, one of Yorkshire's great houses. The Trust disposed of many items in the house by holding a sale at Christies. The *Yorkshire Ridings Magazine* carried a report on the sale.

Every London dealer was represented, many commission bids were left and telephone bids came in from all parts of the country and overseas. There were 761 lots covering furniture, works of Art, prints, maps, ceramics and garden statuary. And for some reason it was an item of statuary that caused the most excitement. Lot 151: A cast stone dwarf, emblematic of war, shown in aggressive stance, holding a musket at his right side, minor damages – 44 inches high. Bidding was brisk and as the breastplate was decorated with the German Imperial emblem it brought some telephone bidding from Germany. The estimate was £700–1,000. It was knocked down to a telephone bidder for an incredible £14,300.

So Fyvie's bargain-price dwarf was taken to his new castle home in the valley of the Upper Ythan. He originally stood at the loch in the grounds of the castle, but he was slightly damaged by a gardener and they took him inside the castle for safety. Now he stands on the great wheel-stair in the castle, keeping a watchful eye on all the people who come to see the marvels of Fyvie. Be careful, however, what you say when you pass him, for any crude jokes about dwarfs and midgets might tempt him to reach for that formidable-looking musket.

5

THE CENTENARIANS

When I was a young reporter I was sometimes sent out to interview old ladies who were celebrating their 100th birthday. It was worth a story and a picture in the paper – scoring a century was something special. It was a day of cards, cakes and kisses. The lord provost would turn up to congratulate the old dears, toasts would be made, and there would be the inevitable telegram from the queen.

Nowadays, the number of royal telegrams must have doubled or trebled, for we are all living much longer, or so they tell us. We are no longer fussed by people reaching their century. We have forgotten the 'three score years and ten' rule that Charles Murray once wrote about, 'Three score an' ten the Lord laid doon the length o' years for laird an' loon, An' noo, wi' sax ayont oor share, we canna look for mony mair.' 'Hamewith', [Homeword as Charles Murray was nicknamed] is the title of one of his poems. He died in 1941 in his late seventies.

So how do we now compare with our forebears in the longevity stakes? In the second half of the eighteenth century, a list published by the *Aberdeen Journal* highlighted what was described as 'remarkable cases of longevity last century'. It showed that in Aberdeen and the north-east at that time there were more centenarians around than anyone could have imagined.

There were seventy-two entries in the list. The first date was 7 March 1749, when Andrew Cumming, Peterculter, died at the age of 102. 'He had the use of all his senses till within two or three days of his death,' it was said. One by one they were counted off: John Jeans, near Old Aberdeen, died on 13 March 1751, aged 104; William Reid, mason, 'upwards of 100', died in December of that year. Unfortunately, John Smith, Esq., of Inveramsay (the only man with Esq. after his name), didn't quite make his century. He was, however, 'nearly 100' and he was given his place in the Roll of Honour.

There were snippets of information with each entry about the centenarians when they chalked up 100 years. It made surprising reading. For instance, William Barnes, Brodie House, was a servant with the Brodie family for seventy years. He was 'upwards of 100' and

'Under this ston lyes . . .' This tombstone is in the kirk yard of St Fergus, which is near the site of the old village of Drumlinie. Today, nothing at all remains of the village; its exact site is unknown.

less than a month before his death, on 23 January 1759, he was 'enjoying a game at fencing'. The following month, Gavin Argo, a blacksmith at Udny, died at the age of 'about 100 years'. He was, it said, 'a powerful man, and retained his strength so long that he was able to work at his forge till a few days before his death.'

But the womenfolk didn't let the old boys have all their own way. Catherine Brebner, from Cairnie, showed that she could outlive and outdo them. She died on 1 February 1762 at the incredible age of 123, and it was said that she retained her senses to the last. During her last winter she was even able to 'engage in spinning'. Then there was Agnes Christie, Midmar, who died three months after Catherine. She was 104 and was 'hale and vigorous to the last'. Agnes cocked a snook at old age when she walked sixteen miles in one day – about two months before her death. Isobel Watt was another centenarian who believed that 'shanks' mare' (one's own legs) would keep her going. She was married for seventy-four years to Robert Williamson, wardhead of Countesswells, who died at the age of ninety-eight, leaving her a widow in her 100th year. The report on 'this remarkable woman' said that when she was 100 she was in such excellent health that she still walked to the markets in Aberdeen to sell her poultry and eggs.

George Keith, Banchory-Devenick, got a good send-off when he died on 1 April 1771. He had thirty-eight children and grandchildren, and fifteen great-grandchildren. When he was buried they all followed his coffin to the grave. But Keith's family paled to insignificance when matched against the family of John Thomson, a labourer from Mundale, near Forres. He was father to forty-five children and grandfather to eighty-six. He was married twice, becoming great-grandfather to ninety-seven and great-great-grandfather to twenty-three. This made it a magnificent total of 251, but there is nothing to show that they all turned out for his funeral when he died on 28 July 1784.

One particular place in the list struck a bell for me – Auchleuchries, Cruden. It was there that Alexander Dickie died in December 1791, at the age of 101. This must have been at the croft at Auchleuchries, where my grandfather, John Murdoch, saw out his days. Both men were twice married. Dickie's wife died in her 105th year, and he married his second wife when he was in his 85th year. My grandmother died at the age of forty-four, and many years later John Murdoch married his housekeeper, Bathia Faith Adie. He died in 1936 at the age of eighty.

Huskers and hawkers, besom makers and beggars, wealthy farmers and well-bred ladies ... people from all walks of life were in the longevity line-up. The huckster was William Auld, from Aberdeen, who died in 1785 aged 101, while another Aberdonian, John Drum, the besom maker, died in the same year aged 103. Elizabeth Gordon, Lady Leuchars, died at the age of 111; she was a relation of the duke of Gordon and great aunt to the earl of Fife.

You wouldn't think that life as a beggar would lead to a ripe old age, but one beggar on the list lived to be 113 – and she was a woman! Her name was Jean Petrie, and she came from Peterhead. She died in June 1798, and the report on her said 'This remarkable woman followed the calling of a beggar and was able to wander through the country till within a few days of her death.' Her father lived to 114.

I found it difficult to decide who in the *Journal* list would have won the centenarian's crown in the eighteenth century. He or she had to have more than just a string of years to claim a place on top of the bill. One of the strongest contenders was 'Charles Leslie, hawker, Old Rain, aged 105.' He died on 7 October 1782, and it was said that 'he was able to prosecute his calling till within a week or two of his death'. Better known as Mussel-mou'd Charlie, Leslie's description as simply a hawker was ill-judged. He was a chapman poet and a ballad singer who was a familiar figure throughout Scotland. They called him 'the street laureate of Aberdeen', and when he died at the age of 105 the 'Bells o' Raine' [Old Rayne] rang a melancholy farewell to him. His portrait hangs in Fyvie Castle alongside those of the lords and ladies he visited during his travels.

There is no doubt, however, that the laird of longevity was Peter Garden, a farmer from the Chapel of Seggat at Auchterless, who lived to the extraordinary age of 131. He lived through ten rulers and sovereigns, starting with Charles I and Oliver Cromwell and running through to George III. He used to say that in his young days he was a 'gey loon' [great rascal]. A painting of him carried the caption 'The Celebrated Peter Garden of Aberdeenshire, famous for uninterrupted health, gigantic stature and longevity, having lived to the uncommon age of 131 years with his faculties entirely to the last.' He worked on his farm until a few years before his death, when his sight failed him.

He married a second wife when he was 120. She had been his servant and married him 'for a bit of bread'.

Oddly enough, there were few Aberdonians in the *Journal* list, and when it appeared in *Scottish Notes and Queries* a contributor wrote in to add a few more names, including a Mary Cameron, who died at Braemar in 1784 aged 129.

Why the eighteenth century was a boom year for the oldies is a mystery, and nobody as far as I know has tried to explain it. But a report in 1785 suggested that reaching your century was not unusual in the north-east at any time. 'Aberdeenshire,' it said, 'hath the reputation of being remarkably healthy, and the inhabitants are distinguished by their longevity.'

6

NOT FOR PURITANS

The *Aberdeen Magazine* of April 1832 gives the following as occurring in Kildrummy,

Heir lyes an honest vertus woman, Janet Forbes spous to Thomas Espler, in Newbiggin, quha departed this lyfe in the yeir of God.

'This weightye stone doth containe
Erth's greatest losse, Hevin's greatest gain,
Her glasse is rune, her time was worthie spendit,
Hir fame stil lives, tho' that her days be endit.'

As remarked by the editor, 'the panegyric here is perhaps a little strained; and some may doubt whether Janet Forbes was "Erth's greatest losse, Hevin's greatest gain".'

There are some people who collect epitaphs as if they were old coins or foreign stamps. There are all kinds of epitaphs – sad, poetic, happy, inexplicable, cruel, curious and downright bizarre. Thomas Espler's lines might be regarded as maudlin. The *Aberdeen Magazine* editor said 'There is reason to believe it was written by her husband after her death, and we must make allowance for the honest man's feelings at such a time.'

Epitaph hunting has been catching on, for there are mountains of booklets giving details of the wording on gravestones, particularly in creepy old kirk yards in rural areas. There are teasers in some of them. In my book, *The Road to Maggieknockater*, I found farms with the name of Fill-the-Cup. I never found out what it meant.

Oddly enough, the first book of epitaphs was published in 1820. It was *The Eccentric Magazine; a Collection of Anecdotes, Epitaphs, Bon Mots. Conundrums, &c &c* by Alexander Laing. 'Stachie' Laing was the gley-eyed packman–poet who wrote *The Donean Tourist* and was one of the first historians on Donside and Deeside.

The turbulent burns and brooding hills of Strathdon were Stachie's stamping ground. He tramped these ancient trails with a box of books on his back, selling them at cottar houses and lairds' mansions. Some said *The Donean Tourist* was almost unreadable, and they may have been right, but there were little gems that I plucked out of it like a magpie pecking at some glittering prize – pieces of history, reports of battles, anecdotes and tales about the lairds.

Although Stachie had written other books, *The Eccentric Magazine* stood out for the wrong reasons, for it was packed with crude epitaphs. He loved to rummage about in ruined kirk yards looking for interesting ones, particularly those with a bawdy or risqué twist or two. *The Magazine* cost one shilling and carried a poetic warning to its readers, 'Not for the Puritan nor Prude These jocund tales took birth, But here are plac'd as Pleasing Food For every Son of Mirth.'

When a woman who had met him was asked what she thought of him (he often lodged in her father's house), she wrote 'He was not a man of much education, but a great reader and well-informed, with a craze for hunting churchyards for old or quaint epitaphs. There must have been something "low" about him, for he sold books to the farm servants that he dared not have produced in the house.'

Coull Church, where 'Stachie' Laing was said to have found an epitaph to 'little Andrew Gray', whose 'conscience was cannon-proof'.
Laing's mother was born at Coull.

Stachie Laing was born in Aberdeen, the illegitimate son of a local advocate; his mother, a domestic servant, was a native of Coull on Deeside. A number of his epitaphs came from Coull, among them this verse about a Mr Andrew Gray,

> Within this narrow House of Clay,
> Lies little Mr Andrew Gray.
> To set him forth requires some skill,
> He knew so little good or ill,
> And that his memory should live
> Some small account I mean to give.
> He had a Kirk without a roof,
> His conscience sure was cannon-proof;
> He was Prelatic First, and then
> Became a Presbyterian.

I searched the stones and never found poor Mr Gray, but time had erased some of the inscriptions. To be fair, many of his epitaphs could be seen and checked, such as the one in Alford about Mary Forbes,

> Within this isle interr'd behind these stones,
> Lyes pious, wise, good Mary Forbes' bones.
> To Balflig daughter, and of blameless life,
> To Mr Gordon, Pastor here, was wife.
> Expiravit, April 27, AD1728.

Apart from the spelling of Balfluig, the epitaph was correct. At the west gable-end of the kirk there is a stone plaque with the dates 1804 and 1826, and underneath it against the wall is the memorial that was mentioned in Stachie's book. On either side of the memorial are two figures in robes, both holding their right hands over their coats, and at the top is the figure of a naked angel (with wings). The author Nigel Tranter described these as 'grotesque stone figures seemingly with bellyache'.

One of the epitaphs in *The Eccentric Magazine* was about a ship's Master who died and was 'bound by the King of Terror's chains'. It sounded like a phrase thought up by Stachie himself, but, in fact, it was frequently used in epitaphs. I remember seeing it in a tablestone in the Cabrach marking the grave of an Alexander Scott, of Aldunie, who died in the 1830s. It carried a chilling message for the living, 'Reader be admonished! You are moving on to meet The King of Terrors.'

I was told of an old man on his deathbed who was asked by the minister if he was ready to meet the King of Terrors. He replied sourly, 'I might well be, for I've lived now for forty years with the Queen of Terrors.'

Stachie, I think, had a fondness for short, sharp explosive epitaphs such as

> 'Here lies my wife, without bed or blankets,
> But dead as a door nail, God be thankit.'

Or this one,

> 'Beneath this stone, a lump of clay, Lies Arabella Young,
> Who, on the twenty-ninth of May, Began to hold her tongue.'

But one wife had her say, 'A Husband's corpse this tomb contains! And I must now my time employ In weeping o'er his sad remains, With ever streaming tears of joy.'

Stachie must have taken his pack to Aberchirder during his travels, for he had a number of epitaphs from the Foggieloan area. Two of them were from Marnoch, where St Marnan's kirk yard has an impressive number of spooky tombs and sepulchral monuments. One of the stones read 'Hear lys the body of Alex Messon [Masson?] who departed this life Jan 6 and of age 88 year 1748.' If the spelling was dubious, it was worse on the stone over the grave where Mr Messon's son was buried. The epitaph read 'His Fader K.G. Massan in Fogglon who departed this life the 22 of April 1782 egged 30.'

Not very far away was the deserted village of Inverkeithny, whose churchyard had a grave where the epitaph had spelling that was a good deal worse, yet it told a sad and pitiful story of what happened to a family there. It read,

> Under this grave ston doth ly intrred in hop of a blesed resurection the
> body of John Faskin who dyed march 12 day 1714 aged to 13 wiks
> Isbl Faskin dyed April of 30 day aged 3 years Alexander Faskin dyed
> november th 1721 aged to 13 wks Elspet Faskin dyed may 8th aged
> to 24 years 1742 Children to John Faskin of Fortry.

Stachie visited a kirk yard at Tarland and reported on two graves. One had been a family burial place for centuries and this is what Stachie said was on the tombstone.

Here lys John Davidson, who was born in the beginning of the present century, lived all his life in Tarland, and died there on the third of March, 1787, going 82 years of age; with two of his children, viz. James and Jean Davidson who died in their infancy; this being the burial place of their family for several centurys. Where many of them are interred, since the first of whom a captain was settled in the country, by the Irvines of Drum, for a particular favour done that family at Edinburgh, in the time of the Stewarts or Scottish Kings. Done by the care of Margaret McCombie The defuncts relict his eldest son John Davidson of Tillychetly, and his daughter Ann Davidson in Tarland, his second son Charles Davidson died in Jamaica some time ago. Praises on Tombs are vainly spent, This defuncts character was an ornament.

The crudest epitaph in Stachie's book was said to come from Aboyne. It went like this,

Beneath this stone in dirty linnen,
Lies the mother of James and Francis Binning,
She lived a Whore, she died a Witch,
So into Hell they hurled the Bitch.
For want of a coffin, she was buried in the girnel,
The earth got the shell, and the Devil the kernel.
All you who wish her name to honour,
Pray stop and read, then piss upon her.

Then there was an epitaph about D—'s godson, 'Here lyes the D—'s godson, Who never lov'd the poor, Hw liv'd like a hog and died like a dog And left what he had to a Whore.'

Stachie Laing, flying stationer, book canvasser and chapman, died in poverty on 20 April 1838, not in Aberdeen, where he was born, but in an old droving inn at Boultenstone on Donside. Drovers, horse dealers, squatters, tinkers, packmen all came to 'Bouties,' as it was called, on their way into the hills. Stachie was well-known there. He was buried in an unmarked grave in the churchyard of Coldstone.

7

MR NISBET'S TWISTERS

Aberdeen has always been fitba daft, drawing thousands of fans to the turnstiles at Pittodrie. Cricket has never had the same impact, some people regarding it as an effete game that slipped over the Border uninvited. It has been called 'the right noble, sterling old English game'. But it hasn't always been like that. Roll back the years and a different picture emerges. In the late nineteenth century, when cricket was a new, rapidly developing sport, football was still finding its feet in Aberdeen. William Skene, author of *East Neuk Chronicles,* published in 1905, had little time for 'that abomination called football'. He said it had crazed the rising generation.

Skene's *Chronicles* first appeared in the *Evening Express* between 1840 and 1860. It was then that he wrote about the games they played on the Links in those days, games with names like smuggle the gig, huntie, staigie, buttons, kee-how, hi-spy, bonnetie kick and bools [marbles]. Seamen from Baltic and American traders laid up in the harbour played at bools on the Barrack Hill. During the winter months the hill became so crowded with players that many of them had to go elsewhere. 'We used to sell them marbles and win them back, very often by cheating, and resell them again and again,' wrote Skene. 'They never complained.'

The Links was also the home of the city's cricketers. Skene wrote about two of the city's crack clubs, the St Nicholas Club and the Union Club – the first consisting mostly of businessmen, the second mainly from the trades.

They were an odd lot. There was Mr Nisbet, a soap boiler and a St Nicholas player, who had a peculiar style of bowling. Batsmen ducked for their lives when 'Nisbet's twisters' came screaming down the pitch. The Union had David Duguid, a fishing-tackle maker, who was a good bowler, Alfred Normable, a currier [someone who grooms horses], Mr Forbes, a blacksmith, and Honest George McKay of the Star and Garter (a pub in Union Street).

Bob Millar, a lithographer, who was 'the most cautious cricketer I ever saw', was generally first in and last out. William Carnie, journalist and author of *Reporting Reminiscences,* who was also a member of the Union Club, said that Millar was the 'deadliest, dodgeist underhand slow bowler seen on the Links'. After a catch, he would send the ball far into the air, thrown up behind his back – 'a kind of juggler feat, difficult and pretty', said Carnie.

But another member of the club, Mr Cay, an old soldier, had an even more exciting trick up his sleeve – or, rather, his feet. When the Union Club were victorious on one occasion, he celebrated by jumping across the canal lock at the Constitution Street bridge. The lock was about thirteen feet broad and there was no room for a running jump, but Mr Cay went flying over like a champion. Skene thought it was 'an exceedingly smart thing to do', but, he added, 'none of Mr Cay's brother cricketers attempted to follow the example', which was not surprising.

The Links was regarded as 'the People's sea-side pleasure ground', the only place open to cricketers, who shared it with golfers. As one pet poet put it, 'Where the brisk and hardy Golfer still Pursues the flying ball, And the merry Cricketer's ringing shout Proclaims the wicket's fall.'

But in 1856 news that the Aberdeen, Peterhead and Fraserburgh railway line was to run through the Links sent a shock wave through the ranks of the bowlers. Carnie said that what followed was 'one of the very fiercest, long drawn-out contests ever experienced'. The matter went to the House of Commons, who gave their decision in favour of the line through the Links. It was said that this would mean 'the destruction of the only Public Park the city possessed'. A huge crowd gathered at a meeting in Castle Street, some carrying placards saying 'Preserve the Links'. George Davidson, a King Street bookseller, trotted out a long poem entitled 'A Lay of the Links', hitting out at those who 'went before the Parliament and sold the people's Links'. These were the Links where gallant pikemen exercised and the Volunteers enrolled and where there was many a grand sham fight on the Broad Hill.

> And o'er the beach and waving bents
> Far as the golden sands,
> The city's joyous thousands thronged,
> In merry laughing bands.
> The city's joyous thousands

Clad in their best array,
Thronged o'er the beach and sandy bents,
And upward where the swelling tents
O'erlooked the sunny bay.

The old men linger on the hill
To breathe the fresh sea gale,
And wives and mothers anxious look
To catch the distant sail.
Where still the honest craftsman
When his hard day's work he drops,
Comes to shun the tempting tap-room
And the fatal tippling shops.
And bands of girls rejoicing
Come trooping o'er the hill,
As the last sound of the evening bell
Is heard from Bannermill.

You hear their merry voices
As they roam from bank to brae
And think with wrath and sorrow keen
That all this gay and gladsome scene
Is doomed to pass away;
And all because of Traitors false
Who did their trust betray.

Skene said that George Davidson got many hearty compliments for his 'unflinching patriotic outburst'. The author was 'a widely respected gentleman – poet, business man, humorist, warm-hearted' and in the 'Lay' he was helped by his 'very clever wife'. But the railway war didn't end there. The directors approached the House of Lords and lo!, said Skene, the standing orders committee of that august body threw out the bill. The Links was saved!

Those were exciting times. There was a song that had this chorus, 'The jolly bat and ball, The merry bat and ball, No sport, say I, 'neath heaven's blue sky Like wicket, bat and ball.'

In 1860 the Aberdeen Club took on a ground professional called Harry Lillywhite. Harry was the first professional who ever came north. According to Carnie, 'old Lillywhite' was one of the 'best underhand slow trundlers' in the game, but it was during his time that fast round-arm bowling became popular. If Bob Millar, the deadliest underhand slow bowler on the rinks, had still been around he would have had to change his style.

The players lived up to the 'merry bat and ball' tag. After a game between Aberdeen and Edinburgh, the players and a few friends dined together in the Lemon Tree Hotel, 'and what a gentlemanly, jovial convocation it was', said Carnie. No doubt today's cricketers are as gentlemanly and jovial as their predecessors, but there have been many changes. Now, a century and a half later, nobody plays huntie, staigie and kee-how on the Links, there are no Baltic traders rolling their bools on the Barrack Hill, and there is no canal which happy cricketers can jump over when they knock up a century. But the Links is still the people's pleasure ground.

8

THE BARDS OF BON-ACCORD

It stands on a shelf above my desk, its title marked out on the spine in plain gilt letters – *The Bards of Bon-Accord*. Now and again I take it down, flip over the pages, and watch the bards come strutting down the years: men like the great John Barbour, with his metrical history of 'The Bruce'; the tailor–poet Deacon Alexander Robb, making merry at Bachelors' Ha'; John Burness, with his immortal 'Thrummy Cap'; and the lesser poets, forgotten rhymesters like Charlie Leslie – Mussel-Mou'd Charlie, the Old Rayne chapman who wrote a ballad telling the world how he bought a wife in Edinburgh for a bawbee. Beside *The Bards* is William Carnie and his three volumes of *Reporting Reminiscences*.

William Walker's book, published in 1877 and spanning the years from 1375 to 1860, has been an indispensable companion to me. I discovered some time ago that I wasn't the only one who felt that way. In *Eminent Aberdonians*, the late Alex Keith mentioned Charles Murray's preoccupation with *The Bards* book. 'In his busy office in South Africa for thirty years,' he wrote, 'and in his wanderings about the world for other twenty, he had near him on his desk or in his luggage one indispensable article, Will Walker's *The Bards of Bon-Accord*.' It was a book, said Keith, that should be on the bookshelf ('however restricted that may be') of every true Aberdonian. 'AK' himself had three copies of the book. One was his own working copy, another a presentation copy which Walker gave to his brother James, who had helped him in its compilation, and the third was Walker's own proof copy with corrections and alterations.

There is no shortage of literary curiosities in the 620 pages of *The Bards,* and the book becomes ever more unusual when you turn the pages to a section headed 'Fugitive Verses and Verse Writers'. Here are the poets who almost made it, and some who had no earthly hope of making it. There are homespun rhymes from characters like Jamie Smith, who dubbed himself the Rhyme-spinner for the hale of Formartine, and a play called 'The Dominie Depos'd', by William Forbes, a Peterculter headmaster, who tells of an intrigue with a young lass 'and what happened thereupon'. Walker said that, although some of the 'fugitive' verses were 'very curious', they were rather poor specimens of verse making. He described a series of poems and songs from a Charles Mitchell, from the Cabrach, as 'a most extraordinary production'. It was very scarce, he said, adding sternly 'and ought to be so'. The only copy he had seen was in the Mitchell Library, Glasgow. 'The coarse chat, courting adventures, smut, &c. that used to go on in a country servants' bothie, put into outrageous rhyme, and in untoned-down language, make up the contents of this curiosity.'

Walker became interested in ballads and folk-songs, building up an impressive collection of traditional works. He was also an avid book collector, and when he died in 1931, aged ninety-one, he had a library of 'many thousand volumes'. It took eight days to disperse them. Today, antiquarian book collectors would pounce on *The Bards of Bon-Accord* like cats on a mouse. Depending on its condition, it would probably be valued at more than sixty pounds. At the beginning of the twentieth century it was selling for less than ten shillings.

Yet those were the glory days of bookselling. In the 1880s, London had the highest number of second-hand bookshops in Britain, Edinburgh was second and Aberdeen came third, followed by Birmingham and Glasgow. The antiquarian bookseller Cliff Milne, whose son Andy opened the Bon-Accord Bookshop in the Spital in 1998, showed me a set of book catalogues dating back to the turn of the twentieth century. One bound volume contained twenty-three catalogues. The average price for a catalogue was three pence. In those days, vast collections of books were auctioned off at sales lasting three or four days. Some, like Will Walker's, lasted for a week or more.

Inside the tightly packed catalogue were to be found the literary treasures of many prominent Aberdonians. Among them was the builder John Morgan, who was responsible for the building of the new Rubislaw House, 'that amazing baroque edifice' as Alex Keith described it, at 50 Queen's Road (see chapter 16). It was in his famous library there that Aberdeen's 'master of stone' filled his bookshelves with books, magazines and photographs, plus a curious array of pamphlets, essays and rectorial addresses, and twenty volumes of the city of Aberdeen accounts.

His library must have been a wonder to behold. Perched on the shelves were the works of local authors like John Hill Burton and A.I. MacConnochie, John Jamieson, with his *Scottish Dictionary*, Sir

Thomas Dick Lauder with his *Great Floods,* a trio of Williams – William Robbie, William Macgillivray and William Carnie – and many, many more, all marching side by side with the old literary giants, among them Scott, Tennyson, Dickens and Stevenson.

There were formidable titles, like *The New Scotch Presbyterian Eloquence and Concordance to the Greek Testament,* rubbing shoulders with *The Keepsake* (five volumes) and *Pencillinngs in Palestine,* and keeping step with *The Works of Rabelais and Boccaccio's Decameran.* There were chapbooks, pamphlets, magazines, music, poetical sketches and literary oddities which were to end up in catalogues as mysterious 'Bundles'.

On the evening of Monday 16 December 1907, the year after Morgan's death, his collection came up for sale at John Milne's auction rooms in North Silver Street. The first night saw 250 lots under the hammer, on the second night the figure jumped to 500, on the third night it rose up to 750, and on the fourth and last night it rocketed to a glorious total of 1,060. Will Walker's *The Bards of Bon-Accord* was there – it was bought for 10s. 6d. There was one particular book that seemed to suit the occasion – *Adventure Among Books.*

John Morgan, who built the new Marischal College, the Aberdeen fish market, the Caledonian Hotel (originally the Grand) and twenty houses in Queen's Road, also had a book in his library which I like to think helped to set him on the road to success. It was illustrated and sold for 2s. 6d. Its title was *How to Build a House.*

Another well-known Aberdonian whose library found its way to John Milne's auction rooms in 1911 was Alexander Munro, the City chamberlain, who in 1896 wrote *Memorials of the Aldermen, Provosts and Lord Provosts of Aberdeen.* His collection included Will Walker's *The Bards,* but its price had dropped to nine shillings. Also on auction was an original sketch by Queen Victoria, 'with letters and photos of Queen's Statue of Aberdeen'. Thirty-four volumes of Spalding Club publications sold for £4 8s. 9d. and thirty-seven volumes of New Spaldings went for £5 12s. 4d.

The setting up of free public libraries at the turn of the century was regarded by many people as the death knell of book collecting, but in 1903 an event took place which made the *Aberdeen Journal* declare, 'The age of book collecting has not passed.' This was the sale of one of the best private collection of books in the north of Scotland; it was owned by the late Alexander Walker, LLD, a city wine merchant. 'From his early years,' wrote the *Aberdeen Daily Journal*, 'everything relating to his native city was of absorbing interest to him. Prosperous in business, with strong literary, artistic and antiquarian tastes, he very early began the genial and educative habit of placing on his bookshelves, or hanging on his walls, choice copies of those works whose authors, subjects or other associations had imparted to them special value in his eyes.'

Walker brought his massive collection together over a period of sixty years. When it went on sale on Tuesday 5 May 1903 the catalogue listed 2,147 lots. In fact, the total number of items far exceeded that figure. The catalogue itself was said to be worth retaining as a record of the event. John Milne certainly thought so, for he upped the price of the catalogue to sixpence a copy.

The book sale was well advertised in advance and national newspapers gave a lot of publicity to it. 'No such collection as this has for many years (in some respects never before) been brought before the public here,' said the *Journal*. It forecast that the sale, which was planned to run for ten nights, would 'prove a memorable one in the auction records of Aberdeen'.

On the evening of 5 May 1903, booksellers and book buyers gathered in the Bon-Accord Auction Rooms to hear John Milne's hammer thump down on Lot 1, 'Abbot, Jacob. The history of Queen Elizabeth. Illuminated title page. Illustrated. Small 8vo. New York 1856.' It sold for 1s. 9d.

It was said that nearly every local book you could think of was in Walker's collection. The first three pages of the catalogue were packed with Aberdeen titles. There were chapbooks, copies of *The Touns Great Bible* (thirty privately printed, 1885), a *Stranger's Guide through Aberdeen,* a brief description of *The Well of Woman Hill,* an Aberdeen Directory, Aberdeen pamphlets and much more.

The *Aberdeen Free Press* reported that there had been a large attendance on the first day of the sale, but the less valuable and more common books were sold comparatively cheaply. 'Rare and good editions of books brought good prices,' it went on. 'The highest figure reached was £2 paid for the edition de luxe of *Johnny Gibb o' Gushetneuk,* with Sir George Reid's plates.' The top figure on the second night was £2 6s. for ten volumes of *Chambers Encyclopaedia*. On the third night the attendance dropped and some books went cheaply, but on the fourth night there was brisk bidding and £5 5s. was paid for an unpublished MS, *Guide to Aberdeen,* by William Kennedy. The auction continued, and the top figure of the ten-day sale came on the eighth night, when £15 6s. was paid for the complete works of W.M. Thackeray. The book sale actually ended on the ninth night, for the tenth night was given over to the sale of antiquities, everything from snuff boxes and medals to three pairs of old spectacles and an ostrich egg.

The most memorable sale in the auction records of Aberdeen ended not with a bang but with a Bundle. The last twelve lots in the catalogue were all Bundles. Lot 2,136 was a 'Bundle containing Jamie Fleeman, Red Letter Saints and 12 others'. Then came a Bundle of *Boy's Own Papers* (fifty monthly parts), a Bundle of school books, a Bundle of university calendars (eight volumes), three Bundles of guide books (fifty-five volumes) and two large Bundles of magazines. Finally, Lot 2,147 wound up the sale with 'Miscellaneous Bundles'.

The age of old-style book collecting has passed, or, at any rate, seldom reaches the heights of yesteryear. The last book auction held at John Milne's auction rooms in North Silver Street took place on 25 June 1981. The catalogue gave the main item as *Scots Unbound and Other Poems by Hugh MacDiarmid*. There were 251 lots. The last was a copy of the Holy Bible dated 1608, translated to English and with 'various pages imperfect and missing'.

So now the ghosts of a century ago look down from the books of my shelves. Among them are names that you can see again and again in the old catalogues: George Walker, who led me through *Aberdeen Awa*; A.I. McConnochie, who took me to the Deeside and Donside hills; Robert Anderson, who once edited my old paper and wrote *Aberdeen in Bygone Days*; and another newspaper man, William Carnie – 'We a' ken Willie Carnie,' they said, 'the mannie's fu o' blarney.'

These were the men whose books were eagerly sought when John Morgan's library was under the hammer – and they are still sought by antiquarian book collectors today.

9

PROPHET OF BETHELNIE

O Bethelnie, O Bethelnie,
it shines where it stands,
And the heather bells around it
shine over Fyvie's lands.

These lines from an old ballad, 'Jeannie o' Bethelnie', no longer ring true, for Bethelnie no longer 'shines where it stands'. Three centuries ago, the parish church of Bethelnie, which lay to the west of the Oldmeldrum–Fyvie road, was the heart of the community. Local lairds were buried there and people came to it from far and wide, but in 1684 the kirk was taken down stone by stone and carried away to a hill at Oldmeldrum, where it was rebuilt.

This happened when the parish's name was changed from Bethelnie to Oldmeldrum, with the result that Bethelnie became a backwater. There was a croft there known as Oldkirk, but the kirk yard beside it became derelict and deserted. Today, the wind soughs through drooping trees encircling it, almost as if to hide the neglect. Rusty, broken railings guard the weather-worn tombstones. It was once said of it 'a more isolated or forsaken spot it would be difficult to imagine'.

At the back of the kirk yard there is a great vault with a heavy oak

The kirk yard at Bethelnie, where 'Doctor' Adam Donald held night-time meetings with his followers.

door held together by iron bands, but it holds no one out. A weathered granite plaque on the lintel of the vault carries a barely readable inscription, 'Beneath this building lie the remains of many generations of Meldrums, Setons and Urquharts of Meldrom AD136–1863.' It is a sobering thought that you are walking on the bones of lairds who carved out the history of this quiet corner.

There are no wreaths at the scattered graves (the last burial was in 1940), no posies of flowers, nobody to say a prayer. It is a sad and lonely place. You would think that no one would visit this abandoned burial ground after dark, but there was a time when one man made regular night-time excursions to it – a curious, goggle-eyed figure who must have scared bairns out of their wits. He had a double chin, long hair and a short neck, and he always stood with his feet apart, his arms hanging loosely in front of him. He held his hands back to back and his long crooked fingers gave the impression that his wrists were partially dislocated. He wore a Kilmarnock cap, a long square-tailed coat with heavy flaps and spreading collar, a waistcoat to match, knee breeches and shoes with buckles.

He was called 'Doctor' Adam Donald, a title he bestowed on him-

Peter Schiveizer outside the vault in the Bethelnie church.

self, and he was known as the Prophet of Bethelnie. People came from far and near to consult him and it was said that 'scarcely anything was beyond the reach of his knowledge'. He was born into an age of superstition, a time when old women were often regarded as witches, and elfs – little folks in green coats – were thought to be 'gweed neighbours'. It was said that when he came into the world in 1703, the son of a Bethelnie cottar, the 'gweed neighbours' carried him away to Elfland and left a changeling in his place.

Whatever Donald was, he had the folk of Bethelnie eating out of his hand. He knew how to play them. If someone consulted him about something lost, his answers were general and cautiously worded so that they scarcely understood what he said, but if the missing articles turned up they would think his mysterious answers had been correct.

Ten years after Donald's death, Dr James Anderson, who edited a literary and scientific magazine called *The Bee* in the 1790s, wrote about the Prophet in his magazine. Unlike Donald, Anderson had a legitimate reason for using the title 'Doctor'; he received a doctorate in law from Aberdeen university in 1780, the year the Prophet died. In an article in *The Bee* he explained what 'Doctor' Donald did when consulted about disorders that had their origin in witchcraft. 'In these cases,' it said, 'he invariably prescribed the application of certain simple unguents of his own manufacture to particular parts of the body, accompanied with particular ceremonies, which he described with all the minuteness he could, employing the most learned terms he could pick up to denote the most common things, so that, not being understood, the persons who consulted him invariably concluded, when the cure did not succeed, that they had failed in some essential particular; and when the cure was effected he obtained full credit.'

The Prophet of Bethelnie, in other words, was an eighteenth-century con man – and a clever one. He couldn't read, but he collected any books he could lay his hands on, particularly 'large books that contained plates of any sort, especially those with woodcuts', which may have impressed his patients. People came from long distances to consult him. His big day was Sunday, when his house was crowded with visitors. His fees were modest – a shilling was the highest fee he charged and if there were no medicines the sum never exceeded six pence. He eventually married and it was said that his wife's superior judgement supplied the defects of his.

'He never,' said Dr Anderson, 'had any friend with whom he kept up a cordial intercourse; he left no sorts of writings behind him; nor have I ever heard of a single sentence of his that was worth repeating – unless it be the four lines of poetry which he desired the painter to put at the bottom of his picture, '"Time doth all things devour; /And time doth all things waste, /And we waste time, /And so are we at last."'

The road to Oldkirk runs past Bethelnie Farm, where I saw a steading with eight white arches – an impressive flashback to the old days. 'It would be nice if there were horses in every arch,' said Vivian Webster, the farmer's daughter. The farmer, William Christie, is now retired. He once said that as a boy he wouldn't have been seen dead near the old kirk yard, especially if he had been made aware of the story of the Prophet of Bethelnie. Now he lives in a splendid house across the road from the farm, and Vivian and her husband Neil are in the farmhouse. Their son Peter has often played in the kirk yard.

North Bethelnie Farm lies farther on, but before that a track cuts off to the right. A sign at the road end says 'Auld Kirk', so I followed it, driving through countryside gleaming with harvest gold. Behind me, the Mither Tap of Bennachie looked down on a scene of peace and tranquillity. Here, Bethelnie was shining where it stood, and I wondered how tales of witches and elfs could flourish in such a setting.

I was stopped by a line stretched across the track, with a building – Oldkirk – beyond it. Striding towards me was Peter Schiveizer, an oil man, who lives there now. 'It's for animals, not people,' he said, and lifted the barrier. I asked where the kirk yard was and he pointed over the dyke beside us. 'That's it,' he said.

If I had been a couple of days earlier I might not have been able to get into it, for he had newly cut the grass and weeds, which had been waist-high, choking the cemetery.

This was where the Prophet of Bethelnie came all alone at suitably eerie hours to converse with departed spirits and to learn from them of 'many things that no mortal knowledge could reach'. At other times he would hold court with his adherents, acting as necromancer or physician, putting them in touch with the dead. Peter told me that there had been a water bucket resting on a stone, where gullible wives would drop in a sixpence so that they could make contact with their loved ones.

According to Dr Anderson, the Prophet had once 'remarked with what a superstitious veneration the ignorant people around him contemplated that uncouth figure he inherited from nature'.

I could imagine him standing there, cracking his crooked fingers, waving his arms, quietly winning over his listeners. 'He affected an uncommon reservedness of manner,' wrote Dr Anderson, 'pretended to be extremely studious, spoke little, and what he said was uttered in half sentences with awkward gesticulations and an uncouth tone of voice, to excite consternation and elude detection.'

I wandered around the kirk yard, peering at the inscriptions on the faded tombstones, mostly from the late eighteenth century. One – in memory of a Thomas Scott and Nan Davie – had crossed hands and roses cut in the granite, another, half hidden in bushes, was erected by Anne Gordon in 'affectionate memory' of her husband George Hunter, who farmed at Easterton and died in March 1867, also their daughter Isabella, who died aged three years. John Duthie, a Bethelnie blacksmith, was buried there and a stone close to the wall of the vault was in memory of John Forbes, Writer in Edinburgh. I would liked to have known more about this fellow scribe, but it gave no more information.

I tried to imagine the kirk yard as it was when there was a church roofed with heather – a building reputed to be of considerable beauty. James Logan, author of *The Scottish Gael*, described the church in his MS notes.

One of the old gravestones in the churchyard.

The ancient structure stood in the north side of the parish, and was about twenty-six paces long and by ten wide. A portion of the site is enclosed by a wall as the burial place of the family of Urquhart. There are few interred here, although the ground is large; and to prevent, as it would appear, its being at all used for this purpose, it is planted over with trees, by which it has a singular aspect.

Logan said there were no gravestones, apart from two small ones, one with the Gordon coat of arms, only about a foot wide and dated 1739, the other with the names of George Gordon and his wife dated 1661 and 1650. However, a third grave was also mentioned – the Prophet's grave. 'The famous Adam Donald,' Logan wrote, 'the prophet of Bethelnie, lived close to the churchyard, in which his grave is seen with the stone on which his water bucket rested, for a headstone.'

There are arguments over the name of the church at Bethelnie. It was said to be derived from the Hebrew Bethelmou, meaning 'House of God', but the majority view was that it came from Bethnathalan, meaning the dwelling of St Nathalan. In this land of green-coated elfs, old ladies branded as witches, and pseudo prophets, Bethelnie's saint added his own touch of eccentricity. When a deadly plague raged around the countryside, St Nathalan decided to crawl round the

Sniffing around the old graveyard is Spike, the young
Peter Schiveizer's pet – a pot-bellied pig.

parish boundaries on his hands and knees beseeching the Almighty to save his people. It seems to have worked, but poor St Nathalan died from exhaustion after completing his marathon crawl. He is said to have been buried in the Bethelnie ground, although it was also claimed that he was interred at Tullich, near Ballater.

For centuries after his death a St Nathalan's Fair was held on 7 January, the saint's day, at Bethelnie. A mighty ash tree – the tree of Parcok or Percock – was planted where he died. There is still a Percok Tree there to-day, but it is a replacement.

As I stood pondering all that had happened at Bethelnie, and how 'Doctor' Adam Donald had left his lurid mark on it, I suddenly saw a pig-like animal grunting and snuffing its way into the kirk yard. It was black, fat, with a huge snout that seemed to sniff out trouble. It wasn't one of the Prophet's unearthly creatures; it was eleven-year-old Peter Schiveizer's pet – a miniature pot-bellied pig called Spike. Spike bored his way past me, gave a contemptuous snort and disappeared. I followed him out, wanting to see the world outside the shattered kirk yard. It seems as if the graveyard will remain unchanged. Peter Schiveizer said the ground was listed and couldn't be touched. He thought, rightly, that that official ruling meant letting it fall back into its wilderness state. He had no wish to disturb sacred land, but he believed that something should be done.

I stood looking over the yellow fields, patterned with the rolls of new-cut hay, stretching away to the Mither Tap. Oldmeldrum lay only a couple of miles away. Back in 1640 it had been a farm town, situated at the intersection of two drove roads, and in 1672 it was created a burgh of Barony. A place of worship was needed and there is a curious story about the 'flitting' of the stones from Bethelnie's kirk to Oldmeldrum. Apparently, the stones were taken to the Hill of Parcock and every morning it was found that they had been moved to the common east of the village. The villagers believed that this was a sign indicating where the church should be and it was erected on the spot where it now stands.

10

LAMENT OF JOHN HOME

When Aberdeen Corporation faced financial collapse in 1817, the pet poets and broadsheet scribblers reached for their pens. To slip into bankruptcy was nothing less than a disaster, a 'huge bungle', they said, which was investigated by the House of Commons, and there were plenty of scribes ready to have a go at the city Fathers. The result was 'a few excellent ballads and songs', but most, if not all, have long been forgotten.

The best was 'The Lament of John Home', which ran to twenty-eight stanzas, each seven lines long. It was full of allusions to well-known local characters, but their names were never disclosed. Some were given first names, others were identified only by their initials. 'The Lament' gives a fascinating glimpse of our 'toon cooncil' two centuries ago. It spares nobody, pointing accusing fingers at 'sleekit', lazy officials, sniping at members who sipped too freely from 'a council board that was aye weel stored', contemplating what happened to 'our auld abstracts'.

As the title indicates, the central character is John Home, keeper of the Town House for more than forty years. He is heard discussing with Simon Grant, the town-sergeant, how the town's bankruptcy had turned their world upside down, and how they might both be 'ruin'd clean' by it. Behind their conversation lay the fear that they would lose all their 'perks', and Home was particularly upset because he would no longer be able to give his old friend some wine from the town's wine cellar.

> Sair, sair's my heart, O ! Symon, man;
> We're ruin'd clean an' a' that;
> Nae nair your wine and congo fine
> Can I gie you, an' a' that –
> An' a' that, an' a' that,
> Your partan [crab] taes, an' a' that –
> The chosen few, an' me an' you,
> Maun shift our 'bodes, an' a' that

The Clerk (1) said, 'John', the ither day,
'Pack up your things, an' a' that;
Baith me an' you, gin a' be true,
Maun leave this house, an' a' that –
An' a' that, an' a' that,
An' C—d (2) ti, an' a' that
Ilk auld kind face, far frae this place,
They'll drive like sheep, an' a' that.'

The Clerk (1) was William Carnegie, the principal town clerk, and C—d (2) was Alexander Cadenhead, advocate, procurator fiscal for the city, and agent before the courts. Home, saddened because he might have to leave the Town House – 'the house where I was fledged' – expressed the hope that Simon, the thief-catcher, would be able to 'spread his claw' over the guilty men responsible for the corporation's downfall. Grant's very name was a terror to evil-doers. With his scarlet, swallow-tailed town-sergeant's coat he was a familiar figure in Aberdeen. When he died he was given a public funeral.

Oh ! Symon, man, you've lang been famed
For catching thieves, an' a' that;
Lord! spread your claw, in D—er's ha' (3)
On that damned crew an' a' that –
An' a' that, an' a' that
On that damned crew an' a' that –
An' a' that, an' a' that
Your H—r—'s, S—ll's (4) an' a' that,
O! grant John Milne (5) a rope may fill
Wi' them, an' mair than a' that.

D—er's ha' (3) was Dempster's Hotel, where the Club held its meetings, and H—r—'s and S—ll (4) were Mr Harvey and Mr Still of Hillden, who were members of the Club. John Home obviously thought that the 'damned crew' who wined and wined in 'D—er's ha'' were partly responsible for the city's ills, but his suggested treatment of them was a bit extreme – he wanted a rope to hang them.

Johnny Milne was the last holder of the post of public hangman in Aberdeen. He took the job in 1805 as an alternative to seven years' transportation for the theft of beehives. In those days, when a criminal was sentenced to death, Johnny was locked up until the execution took place in case he made himself scarce at the last minute.

He was 'a very poor hand at an execution' and had to be helped by officials and others. At one hanging he got into such a state of excitement that a minister had to adjust the rope round the culprit's neck. He had to be pulled off the drop or he would have gone down when the bolt was drawn. Johnny had a miserable life, for as well as hanging people, and making a mess of it, he had a wife who had a wild tongue and a liking for the bottle.

Keeper Home told Simon Grant who he thought should be taken to the scaffold. The first was a 'hungry-looking brat' who 'clashed and sclaved' [gossiped and slandered] when he was on the council,

> There's yon teem, hungry-looking brat (6)
> That clashed and sclaved, an' a' that,
> Fan he was here the ither year,
> A councillor an' a that –
> An' a' that, an' a' that,
> O' our bits an' sups an' a' that,
> He raised a sough [fuss] wi' Johnny Booth (7);
> They'll baith get h—ll, an' a' that.

The 'hungry-looking brat' (6) was Alexander Bannerman, who was secretary to the Club. He became a member of the council in 1811 and later MP for the city, which he represented for thirty years. He was knighted and was appointed lieutenant-governor of Prince Edward Island, governor of the Bahamas, and, finally, governor of Newfoundland – not bad, you would think, for a 'teem, hungry-looking brat'. John Home's dislike of him would have stemmed from the fact that Bannerman chaired many of the meetings which condemned the town council.

'He raised a sough wi' Johnny Booth' (6). This was John Bailie Booth who was editor of a paper that gave its name to a street off Queen Street – Chronicle Street, later Chronicle Lane. This was the *Aberdeen Chronicle*, which cost sixpence [two and a half pence] and found its readers among the less wealthy. The city's bankruptcy brought strong demands from the *Chronicle* for municipal reform. 'Johnny Booth's paper', as it was always known, lasted until 1832, when it 'quietly passed away'.

Two of Simon Grant's men, Richard Merchant (8) and Robert Cantly (9), came under fire in 'The Lament'. Merchant was a town-sergeant and collector of local taxes. Cantly, also a town-sergeant, attended the Public Soup Kitchen, then in St Mary's Chapel, and oversaw the disposal of the soup to the poor. He would have known Willie Godsman, a beggar who was tramping the streets hawking another 'bankruptcy' ballad called 'Last Speech and Dying Words of the City of Aberdeen'. The magistrates took offence at this and banned him from the Soup Kitchen. Deacon Alexander Robb, tailor and satirical poet, wrote a piece called 'Willie Godsman's Lamentation for the Loss of his Broth', which Willie sang through the streets, with the result that the ban was lifted.

These were the verses about the two town-sergeants.

> There's Ritchie (8), that warkhouse loon,
> Sae skeekit, sly, an' a' that,
> Wi' summoning an' poinding [impounding]
> He's done right weel, wi' a' that –
> An' a' that, an' a' that,
> The taxes ti, an' a' that-
> Now viper-like, the hand does bite
> That brought him up, an' a' that.

> An' Rob the muckle lazy folp (9) [term of abuse]
> Wi's brosy [belly] wame an' a' that;
> He was nae fed upo' deaf nits,
> I ken that weel, an' a' that –
> An' a' that, an' a' that,
> The draps o' drink, an' a' that
> We're at our will to tak' our fill,
> The cham'er cats, an' a' that.

> Bit Bob's grown fat wi' draps o' drink.
> The beggar's broth, an' a' that;
> O! sair I wis that things may change,
> Lat's roar again, an' a' that –
> An' a' that, an' a' that

The pickings, man, an' a' that –
Does weel wi' us, an' a' our kind,
An' keeps us snug, an' a' that.

George Shand (10), assistant to the dean of guild officer, who used to visit the markets 'in quest of light butter', was obviously working a 'fiddle' that 'helpit him, an' a' that'.

That saucy rascal, Geordie, ti (10)
Wha cabb'd [pilfered] the wives, an' a' that,
That sowny butter brought to town,
Or scrimp o' weight, an' a' that –
An' a' that, an' a'that,
The butter, man, an' a' that –
It's a fattening thing, as weels the drink,
That helpit him, an' a' that.

The next two verses are about the man who was at the centre of the town's financial crisis, James Hardie (11), the city chamberlain. John Home has the chamberlain in mind when he tells Symon that 'buiks ... are unco guid to mak' a sham.'

An' H—d—e (11), ti, for keepin' buiks
Had wale [choice] o' pounds, an' a' that;
An' yet I doubt they war to mak'
Fan the song got up, an' a' that –
An' a' that, an' a' that,
The want o' sleep an' a' that,
In makin' books to please the crew.
'S near H—d—e felled, an' a' that.
Buiks, Symon, man, are unco guid
To mak' a sham, an' a' that;
But that infernal, cursed crew
Cries 'balance them', an' a' that –
An' a' that, an' a' that,
Wi' sherry, port and a' that,
Aft Bailies spak', wi draps o' that,
Like Solomons, an' a' that.

Bob, the town-sergeant, with his 'draps o' drink', Simon Grant, with his 'wine and congo fine', councillors with their 'bits and sups', bail-lies with 'draps o' that' speaking like Solomon … all through 'The Lament' there are hints of members and officials living it up or 'on the make' at the expense of the civic purse. It was, as someone once wrote, the age of conviviality. There was an old verse which said that at the council table 'the wheels are aye kept tight and greasy, and councillors ride soft and easy'.

The last two verses of 'The Lament' look at the 'auld abstracts' and John Home and his colleagues pray – 'for weel we may' – that things may change.

> They're cracking now, O statements true,
> O' reading, counts an' a' that;
> It's naething like our auld abstracts,
> By whilk we happit a' that –
> An' a' that, an' a' that,
> The town's accounts an' a' that
> Our Bailies keep it wi' themsel',
> For paper, pens, and a' that.

> Then let us pray, for weel we may,
> That things may change an' a' that,
> An' ilk ill thing frae Hadden's hame
> Be far awa' an' a' that –
> An' a' that, an' a' that,
> The guid auld path, an' a' that;
> We yet may sing, till echoes ring,
> Our Borough's close, for a' that.

Under the close-borough system, the town council, like many other councils, was controlled by a small exclusive group of people. The burgesses of guild in Aberdeen passed a resolution which 'attributed the present disaster to the bad system under which the burgh had been governed by the town council being self-elected, and to its administration having become the inheritance of a few individuals who formed a secret junta'. In September 1817 a number of magistrates and councillors passed a similar motion which said that the absence of checks on the burgh's constitution had led to the 'heavy calamity which has befallen it'.

So who were the 'few individuals' in the secret junta? The answer lay in the lines of the John Home song, where the keeper of the Town House prayed that things might change – 'and ilk ill things frae Hadden's hame be far awa'.' The Hadden family, prominent textile manufacturers, held sway between 1798 and 1819, led by two brothers, Provost James Hadden and Provost Gavin Hadden, who had the office of lord provost between them for half the period, from 1801 to 1832.

There were allegations that the Haddens 'kept their seats warm for family successors', for over the years a number of their relatives and friends held council posts of one kind or another. In 1819, a report on burgh reform said that James Hadden had been fifteen times on the council, a business partner, Provost Alexander Brebner, had been ten times, while many members were 'chiefly either relations or connections in business with Provost Hadden' and his brother Gavin. Ten times Provost Alexander Brown, a local bookseller, was a Hadden supporter and was in the civic chair for two terms.

Note: The parliamentary report on the Aberdeen corporation's insolvency said,

> According to the uniform and immemorial practice of the borough, a statement purporting to be an abstract of the accounts of the corporation was exhibited and read to the burgesses at annual head courts at Michaelmas, for the avowed purpose of informing the inhabitants of the state of the town's affairs. But it appears from (Mr Hardie's) evidence that these statements, as long as he could remember, never did exhibit, and never were really intended to exhibit, a statement of the money affairs of the town.

In each statement, from the year 1800 up to 1812, an account was entered of the town's debts. Thus in 1810 the debt of the borough was stated to amount in whole to £6,874 17s. 4d., while, in fact, the debt was about £140,000 or £150,000; and from 1813 to 1817 no account of debt whatever was entered in the annual statement as owing by the town.

11

A MIRACLE CHURCH

When I first saw the kirk of Knockando perched on a hill above the River Spey, its white bell tower gleaming in the sun, I thought of the church – the original Knockando church – that had stood there nearly two and a half centuries ago. It must have been no less picturesque, but in a different way, for it had a fine thatched roof. The churchgoers would have been proud of it, but they were also careless, for they let the thatch grow and grow and grow until it became so heavy that the roof gave way and collapsed.

In 1757 a new church was built, but nobody could have foreseen that in the long years ahead history would repeat itself. In 1990 the roof collapsed again, shattered by a fire that devoured almost the whole building. They said that a mouse had eaten through a wire and started the blaze, but whether or not the wee, sleakit, timorous beastie was at

The Kirk of Knockando, perched on a hill above the River Spey.

fault is anybody's guess. I met Mrs Ella McKidd in the kirk yard and she told me that this story was going the rounds at the time.

Ella, who stays in Elgin, had come through to Knockando with her husband to put flowers on her parents' grave. She told me about the fire, and promised to send me newspaper cuttings about it, and pictures, and also a video with a film taken on the night. True to her word, she sent the video and I sat and watched the death throes of the kirk, flames leaping through the shattered windows, firemen silhouetted against the glare of the fire.

That fire gutted a church that was said to be the loveliest in the country, with a distinctive tower that helped it to make it a well-known landmark. The Rev. Robert Prentice, who was minister for forty-one years, said the church always reminded him of a French chateau.

Nobody expected to see yet another church springing up on the Knockando hilltop, but out of the ashes came a new kirk – a kirk for the twenty-first century, with an impressive new tower. It was still the loveliest kirk on Speyside, better than the last perhaps, and beautifully planned and constructed. It stood there among the ancient tombstones, looking down on a watch-house where elders once kept a lookout for body snatchers. The watch-house had become a sanctuary where people could rest from the toils of the outside world. 'Meditate and pray', it said, and it seemed as if that was what the Knockando folk had been doing.

The interior of Knockando Kirk.

I got the key for the door of the church and went inside. 'God saw that it was good,' said the inscription on a stained-glass window. I peered into the bell tower and then climbed the stairs to the gallery and looked down on the pews, which ranged towards the pulpit in a V formation, as if drawing the minister and congregation nearer to each other.

I went outside and looked up at this extraordinary building, wondering at the 'miracle' that had happened in the wake of that terrible fire. I wanted to know more about this tiny community, about the folk who had set out to build such a church when kirks all over the country were hearing the clash of kirk doors as congregations abandoned them.

Knockando takes its name from *cnoc cheannachd*, hill of commerce, market hill, but much of the commerce today carries the reek of whisky. I found that part of its story was tucked away in a memorandum written by John G. Shand, a local man who went off to London and joined the police force. Fifty-four years later he came back to revisit his home country and to put on paper his thoughts about Knockando and its folk. It covered the years from 1887 to 1955. He went to the 'new church' and noted that the old church was of different construction, the steps leading to the galleries being built on the outside of the church.

A painting of the old church, which was burned down.

'The church bell was rung by the bellman (Willie Taylor) who stood outside the northern gable exposed to all weathers. He was however in a good position to pass the time of day with those who were entering for the service. There were two Willie Taylors in the parish, Willie the bellman and gravedigger and Willie Mole, the hangman or mole catcher, a noted worthy who ended his eventful life at or near Blackhillock about 1911. He was at one time a coachman about Balmoral Castle in the reign of Queen Victoria, but when I knew him he was earning his living as mole catcher, with occasional spells as a gillie at Knockando House when the shooting season was on. He was a man of intelligence who had rather a high-pitched voice and somewhat given to drinking not wisely but too well. His favourite expression when in his cups and on his way home was 'Steady the boat noo, Willie.'

John G. Shand was born at Mannoch Cottage, to the north, of Upper Knockando, where his father was gamekeeper. At the start of his nostalgic tour he called in at the smiddy, where the school bairns used to watch the sparks fly. The old fireplace and anvil were still there, but there was no smell of singeing horses' hooves.

He ran across old Peter Bremner, the retired blacksmith for Crofthead, near Cardow, where Peter often went for 'burnt ale for his coos and stirks'. He carried the ale in two pails suspended from a wooden shoulder brace. 'The quantity of ale in the pails was a good indication of the amount of whisky Peter had imbibed,' wrote John. 'If the buckets were full Peter was completely sober, but if they were empty then Peter was fou [drunk].'

John and his father often went down to a store at Gracemount, using a pony and cart. When there, they bought food for the sporting dogs – John kept twenty to thirty for the shooting tenant.

One of the great events of the year was the farmers' annual hare hunt. The tenant of Knockando House gave them a snack lunch and six bottles of whisky. The farmer at Clashindarroch, William McDonald, better known as 'Red Wull o' the burn', was a familiar figure at the hare hunts. An eccentric man, short, paunchy, with a thick patch of red hair running round behind his ears, he used an old muzzle-loading gun and black powder. He always went down on one knee to fire at a hare. The hare usually escaped, but the black powder caused such a smoke that Wull disappeared from view for a few minutes.

Warm, friendly people drift through the pages of John G. Shand's memorandum: for example, old Jessie Smith, who ran the shoppie next to the smiddy, selling sticks of 'long John' or barley sugar to the bairns; and Mrs Lewis Cumming, an 'astute and dear old lady' who took John in when he delivered a present of game from the shooting tenant of Knockando House, saying to him 'Come awa' in laddie and hae a piece. Yer teeth are still langer than yer beard.' The Younies lived in Windmill Cottage; the windmill provided power for the adjoining carpenter's shop. 'On Brose and Bannock Day,' wrote John, 'his mother and sisters made us bairns welcome as it was always our first house of call.'

The East Mains was tenanted by John Smith, better known as John Moses. He got that nickname when he was tenant of the Leakin Farm at the Hill Foot. While at the Feeing Market at Aberlour a friend hailed him with the query, 'Hullo John, how are ye doing at the Leakin?' John replied 'Oh, just like Moses in the wilderness.' Moses it was ever after.

Through the woods was a small township called Dalmunack, which in 1900 consisted of about twelve or more houses, each with a small bit of land attached to it. The first house was occupied by Sailor Jack, who had been in the Royal Navy. He was killed by a goods train near the Knockando siding about 1906. John McDonald, the oldest inhabitant in the parish, also lived in Dalmumack. He was said to have walked to the church and back, a distance of eight miles, on his ninety-second birthday.

John's visit to Knockando wasn't his last to this Shangri-la on the Spey. He came back 'for another jaunt round the parish in another airt', making up, perhaps, for all the years he had lost.

12

THE COW'S HAUGH

'It was called the cow's haugh – a name to mark a lovely setting. The word 'haugh' means level ground on the banks of a river, and in this case it was where the Water of Avon met the Spey. Here, Ballindalloch Castle was built – 'the perfect picture of a Highland castle', wrote the historian Dr W. Douglas Simpson.

This imposing building had developed from a fortalice of the sixteenth century, and was greatly altered and enlarged in 1845 in the castellated style. The date 1546 is carved on a stone lintel in one of the bedrooms – proof that the castle, which has been called the Pearl of the North, goes back more than four centuries.

Ballindalloch has been the family home of the Macpherson-Grants since 1546, one of the few privately owned castles to have been lived in continuously by its original family. The present laird is Claire Grant-Russell, who with her husband, Oliver Russell, carries on the ancient traditions while continuing to improve the castle and the estate. They are a friendly couple, known for making visitors welcome.

The castle is one of the most beautiful in Scotland and it has a wonderful setting to match, being surrounded by hills and by the waters of the mighty Spey and Avon flowing through the grounds. There is a beautiful rock garden with tumbling spring water, laid out in 1937 by the Fifth Baronet, and a wall garden which was redesigned in 1996 to celebrate the castle's 450th anniversary.

But if an ancient tale is to be believed, Ballindalloch Castle should never have been built on the cow's haugh – the original plan was to build it farther up the river on higher ground at a spot known as the Castle Stripe, from which a vast panorama of Speyside can be seen. It was regarded as the strongest site, but a series of eerie events made the laird change his mind.

When work began on the castle, what was built during the day was blown down during the night. It happened when the clock struck twelve, a sudden tempest swept down from Ben Rinnes and carried the building materials headlong into the Spey. It stopped as suddenly as it began and when quietness descended on the scene an unearthly laugh was heard, echoing down the hill.

This happened a few times and the laird, believing that it was the work of a neighbour, decided to keep watch himself. Midnight struck and the wail of a rising tempest could be heard. It came howling down like a thousand demons, lifting the laird and his henchman off the ground and down the hill until they were caught in a large holly tree. It ended suddenly, as before, and a wild laugh filled the air, followed by a voice saying 'Build in the cow haugh! Build in the cow haugh!' Then silence fell on the scene.

The laird, realising that some unseen power had been warning him against building on the Stripe, abandoned his plans and built his castle on the cow haugh, which was then a marshy site. As it happened, a marshy site would have been just as defensively effective as the original choice. So out of that marsh came the castle and estate, free from demons, that is known today as the Pearl of the North.

Note: One of the *Biggles* books written by Capt W.E. Johns was set in the vicinity of Ballindalloch Castle (see chapter 13).

Ballindalloch Castle, 'the perfect picture of a Highland Castle', built in the cow's haugh.

13

BIGGLES FLIES IN

Where the mighty Spey comes tumbling down through the Banffshire landscape on its way to Ballindalloch Castle it passes an old Victorian family house standing sedately on the banks of the river. It is called Pitchroy Lodge and it is now a luxury howff for fishers testing their skill on one of the most famous salmon rivers in Scotland.

For some, however, the name Pitchroy has another meaning, for it was from there that a famous aviator took to the skies some sixty years ago. His name – Biggles.

The story of James Bigglesworth, DSO, DFC, MC really begins in Tomintoul, the village that Queen Victoria said was 'the most tumble-down, poor-looking place I ever saw'. I went there to find out about Biggles creator, Capt. W.E. Johns, the man who made the fictional Biggles a hero to thousands of youngsters. He was a First World War flier and author of a long list of *Biggles* books, and he had two great interests – fishing and flying.

Pitchroy Lodge, where Capt. W.E. Johns wrote many of his Biggles books.

The reason I had him in my mind in Tomintoul was that I had been told by a friend, Sandy Pringle, that when he was on holiday there as a boy he met Capt. Johns. Johns was staying in the Richmond Arms Hotel, where he spent the summer writing his Biggles books. He drew a quick sketch of one of his aeroplanes and signed it for his young admirer.

William Earl Johns' story might have been plucked from one of his own books. Born at Bengeo in Hertfordshire in 1893, William was the son of a tailor, and joined the Territorial Army – the King's Own Royal Regiment – in 1913. When war broke out he was sent to Gallipoli to fight the Turks. Later, he was transferred to the Machine Gun Corps and sent to Salonika in Greece, where he had a grim taste of life in the trenches. In 1917 Johns put in for a transfer to the Royal Flying Corps. He trained in a Maurice Forma Shorthorn aircraft and in 1918 was posted to a bombing squadron in Azelot, near Nancy in France.

He flew in the De Havilland DH4 aircraft nicknamed 'flying coffins' because the petrol tank was between the pilot and his rear observer, making it an ideal target for enemy aircraft. Johns took part in many bombing raids and as the war drew to an end he was shot down on a raid to Mannheim and taken prisoner.

Out of his war experiences came the daredevil flier who was to capture the imagination of the nation's youth: Major James Bigglesworth, DSO, DFC, MC – in other words, Biggles. Although James Bigglesworth was a fictional figure, his biography was mapped out in the books Capt. Johns wrote, among which were *The Boy Biggles and Biggles Goes to School*. His role in the First World War was dealt with in such books as *Biggles of the Camel Squadron* and *Biggles Flies East*. His hunt for lost treasures in South America, his spell in the RAF during the last war, his work with the police force, his flights 'down under' in Australia and much more filled the barrage of books carrying Biggles' name.

Capt. Johns' link with Tomintoul was forged in 1944 when Duncan McNiven, owner of the Richmond Hotel, invited him to spend a fishing holiday there. Tired of living in London during the air raids, weary of doodlebugs and V2s, Johns jumped at the chance. 'Enemy action at last forced me to abandon my home,' he wrote. He went north to 'match my wits against those of the Avon salmon'. It was the first of many trips to Tomintoul and it was there that he wrote *Biggles and the Poor Rich Boy*. The setting for this book was the hill country around Tomintoul. The Richmond Hotel, which Johns made his headquarters for the summer, was mentioned frequently in the book, as was Tomintoul itself and the surrounding countryside

Biggles and the Poor Rich Boy was the story of how in this wild country Biggles helped to track down a kidnapped boy, Carlo Salvatore, son of a multimillionaire, snatched away by Cesare Paola, a man with a grievance against Carlo's father. Interestingly, Biggles' search took him over an area which saw a real live manhunt. Percy Topliss, an army deserter who murdered a London cab driver, fled north to Scotland and hid out in an old cottage by the Conglass Water in the Lecht. When the police tracked him down, a gunfight took place and two policemen were wounded. In 1986, a TV film about the Topliss drama was made by the BBC.

Johns' visits to Tomintoul whetted his appetite for the Highlands. Queen Victoria may have seen the village as a tumble-down, poor-looking place, but Biggles' creator fell in love with what he called 'the serene heart of the Highlands of Scotland'. In 1947 he rented Pitchroy Lodge. It was, he said, 'in a remote glen where no man goes from one year to another'. Here, he fished to his heart's content and held regular shooting parties for his friends.

But it wasn't all fun and games. As he cast his line in the sparkling waters of the Spey, he was thinking of new flights and new adventures

The Richmond Hotel, Tomintoul, where Capt. Johns stayed while in the area.

for his hero. Johns wrote fifteen books in his six or so years at Pitchroy, some in the lodge, others in a fisherman's hut by the river. Ballindalloch Castle came under his pen. It was the setting for a non-Biggles book, *Where the Golden Eagle Soars*. He also wrote short stories and articles and a science fiction space series set in an Inverness castle. During the winter he usually went to France to escape the Scottish climate, returning in mid-March. In 1953 he went south to live at Park House, Hampton Court. He died in 1968.

I went to Tomintoul in search of Biggles, or at least for some link with the intrepid flier and the man who created him. Tomintoul has come a long way since Queen Victoria slandered it. She saw it as merely 'a long street, with miserable dirty-looking houses and people, and a sad look of wretchedness about it'. Today, guidebooks mention the 'one long street with a square in the middle' but add that it makes a perfect village green, and the countryside around the village has been described as 'enchantingly beautiful'.

When Alexander, fourth Duke of Gordon, drew up a plan for a new village – the Town of Tamantoul – in 1776 he obviously had in mind the visitors who would come to this 'enchantingly beautiful countryside' for he gave an instruction that there should be a 'right Publick house for the accommodation of Travellers'. There were three inns in Victoria's time.

The River Spey, where Capt. John fished during his stay at Pitchroy.
He wrote some of his books in the fishing hut by the river.

Whisky, of course, has always featured largely in the minds and mouths of Tomintoul folk. The *Statistical Account for Scotland* in 1794 said of the folk of Tomintoul, 'All of them sell whisky and all of them drink it.' Look in the window of a shop in the 'long street' and you might think that some imbibed too much. Here, a prostrate figure lies clutching a bottle and breathing heavily – a rubber 'drunk' made life-like by pumping air into it so that its chest heaves.

The shop is called the Whisky Castle and its shelves are packed with every whisky you can think of – and a few you would never dream of. Mike Drury, the owner, says there are 300 different whiskies – all Scottish. Mike, a chef and restaurateur from Devon, came north to Tomintoul in 2003 to take over the Whisky Castle and Highland Market, a business said to have been established more than a century ago. The blessed aroma of whisky drifts over the old town of Tamantoul and the Whisky Castle helps to keep the Duke of Gordon's 'Travellers' happy.

Tomintoul has an interesting museum, yet one thing is missing – Biggles! I thought that Tomintoul might have paid some modest tribute to Capt. Johns, who came north to write the books that enthralled thousands of youngsters. But I was wrong – no small corner in the local museum nor anyone in the Richmond Arms could tell me about the time Johns stayed there. There were no Biggles books in the local library – or any other library I tried. Few people even knew about Capt. Johns. The sad fact was that Major James Bigglesworth, DSO, DFC, MC had been forgotten.

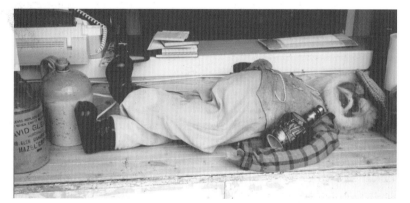

This drunken Highlander lies in the window of the Whisky Castle, the Tomintoul shop run by Mike Drury.

14

JOHN ROW'S DIARY

They say that small is beautiful. Up on a shelf in my room is a tiny Bible, four inches long and two inches wide. It belonged to my mother, Lizzie Murdoch, and I wrote about it in my book, *The Road to Maggieknockater*. Not long after that I came upon another small book, not a Bible but a diary. It dated back to the seventeenth century and was even smaller than Lizzie Murdoch's Bible, being three inches by three inches.

This midget diary proved that small *was* beautiful, for it was crammed full of information: births and deaths; the discovery of witches and warlocks; weather reports; news of a Chapel of Garioch man drowning in the Urie; the murder of a Mar laird, the death of 'the Marques of Montrose, son to James Graham (the great)'; and much more.

The diarist was John Row, principal of King's College, Aberdeen, from 1652 to 1661. He was also a poet and historian and in the words of another historian, John Spalding, 'an arch Covenanter'. In 1863 the Diary was published in *Scottish Notes and Queries,* with an introduction by Aberdeen's city chamberlain, Alex M. Munro.

'This little book, to which the perhaps pretentious title of Diary is given,' wrote Munro, 'is unfortunately incomplete, as it commences on page 59.' The missing pages covered the stormy years in which the 'arch Covenanter' walked side by side with the fiery covenanting minister Andrew Cant. On one occasion they took refuge in Dunnottar Castle, from which 'they fled like foxes'.

Alex Munro thought it 'a matter of great regret' that the early part of the Diary went missing, for it would have formed 'a suitable and welcome continuation of the *History of the Troubles* by Spalding'. Nevertheless, what was left added up to a fascinating record of life in Aberdeen in the seventeenth century. It was written in what Munro called 'beautifully small calligraphy'. He thought that the amount of matter contained was 'wonderful'.

Much of it dealt with births, deaths and marriages. Births usually carried the phrase 'brot to bed': for instance, 'Grisell Row my third daughter was brot to bed of a second son called John Anderson Nov 18 1667 Thursday.' With deaths, Row usually inserted a word or two to about the deceased: Margt Skene, who was 'removed by a violent colick' in 1664, was 'a precious woman'; Bessie Cruikshank, spouse to a merchant burgess of Aberdeen, who died in 1663, was 'a wicked woman'; while Marjorie Moire, wife of dean of guild Thomas Mitchell, who died in 1664, was 'a precious godly woman'.

There was nothing precious or godly about his report on a probationer, Robert Reid, who often preached at Aberdeen. Row disliked him because he had written 'a lying scandalous pasquill [satire] in verse'. Somebody apparently remarked that he 'had too much fanatick blood in his head'. By a cruel coincidence, the probationer was stricken by a sickness that 'issued at his nose, mouth, eyes and ears, all at once a great quantitie of blood, and he bled to death'.

The long roll-call of births, deaths and marriages was relieved by the appearance of witches and warlocks, an eerie tale of people riding on witches' brooms and skulls. This took place in Lothian and Fife, not in Aberdeen, but it was rife in the parish of Liberton, where Row's friend Andrew Cant was minister, so he put it down in his Diary.

In the years '60, '61, '62 a great discoverie of witches and warlockes in Lothian and Fyffe and some other parts; very many in Libberton pariosh; where Mr And. Cant is minister; be east Mussilburg a whole landwart toune all devills, which came to be noticed by a child seven years of age relating very pounctually what was done at the Kings coronation, telling the B. B. (bishops) habit, and mouchs &c, affirming on the morrow to a landwart man that he was present at the coronatione; being asked how came he home so soone, so great a jurney: Ans mother rode on the cat, my father rode on the bissom, I was carried in the skull, and this being revealled they and their neighbours seized upon all confessed.

This rather confused passage was followed by mention of a minister, Thomas Coper, 'dying of grieff' because his wife was 'being deemed for a witch'. 'Also,' wrote Row, 'there is one at Brechin who hath a familiar spirit; and quhen ye come in to hir house ye need to speer nothing at her: She tells you all unasked; as quhat money is in your pocket, your cariage with your wife &c.'

Auld Nick and his warlocks must have been at work in 1696 when two great storms struck Aberdeenshire. The Diary recorded these tempests, first a storm of rain lasting until the last day of November, followed by a great storm of snow. It raged on till 23 December 'without any braick'. One man was

> sent to Logie old toun in the parish of Achterless upon the 26th day of Deer, he said when he came home he did speak with hirds [herds] keeping ther sheep from there corns and had done it all the storm and about the 6 or 8 of Januar they who had ther corns the furth did begin to shear and thresh them and did maick meall of them which was as sweet as if it had been mixed with sugar.'

People from all walks of life stalked through the pages of John Row's Diary: merchants; labourers; goldsmiths; parsons; advocates; people like Robert Downie, who was 'bibliothocaries in the College; the poor and the wealthy; old Davie Riccart, from Aberdeen, who was 'a rich man', and Tipperties Innes, who was a humble servant.

But Row leaned towards what he called 'the better class', well-to-do gentlemen with curious names and some with curious titles: My Lord Banff, surnamed Ogilvie; Robert Fercharson laird of Innercald [Farquharson of Invercauld]; the laird of Ludwharn, elder, surnamed Keyth, who was removed [died] March 1666; and Sir George Mowat of Mowatstoun, alias Ingleshtoun alias Rottenraw in West Lothian. Then there was Robert Dalgleish, 'a tertian in King's Colledge of Abd, and one of my scholarss in Hebrew'; a bursar, a gentleman's son near Selkirk, died in the sea washing himself by hazarding to go too far in.

As for the ladies, Row had nothing but praise for them, or for most of them. He said of Jean Bancanquall, relict of Mr Murray 'at the Cash neare to the kirk of Stramilgo', that she was 'an holy prudent zealous knowing Christian', while Marjorie Innes, relict of Alexander Ferchar [Farquhar] was 'a choise good woman'. My ladie Kilpunt, sister to William Earle of Marshall, 'lived long distracted yet is reported to have died without distraction'.

There were grim tales told about some of the candidates for John Row's little book. The laird of Birness, for instance, was stabbed by a Newtoun Gordoun, so he struck back and 'gored him doun', and Sir

Archibald Johnstone, Lord Waristone, who 'was executed at Edz., first hanged, then beheaded, and his head set up on the Nether bowe beside Mr James Guthrie's head'.

Most of the entries were confined to two or three lines, but one of his longer pieces dealt with George Davidson of Pettens, a chapman who became an Aberdeen burgess and gave money and lands to build a kirk at Newhills. The story has come down through the years and is well known today, but this is how Row told it.

> George Davidson of Pettans and Newhills burges of Abd. Deceased June 16 1663; he guarded foottie Kirk-yaird with a dyck of stone and lyme: Built a bowe-bridge over bucksburn, two miles from Abd. in the highway to Kintor; for when he was a chapman he saw a man droun there, whereupon he vowed to build a bridge over that burn, if ever the Lord did enable him to do it. He mortified 600 merks per annum to a minister at the kirk of Newhills, which kirk he builded; assigning also glebe manse and pasturage to that minister who was to serve the cure there: that as north Don syde was accomodat by the Kirk of New Machar, so south Don syde might be accomodat by the New Kirk of Newhills; the whole parish of old being twelve myles in length, from the bridge of Dee to above Straloch: and lastly he mortified to the toun of Abd. 1,000 lib per annum for to defray one of their three ministers' stipends. Item he left mortifications to the kirkwork to both hospitals to the pore of the town of Abd. for maintaining footie kirk dycks, and the bridge which he caused build over Bucksburn; was buried June 18 at the west kirk style, where a tomb is to be reared over him.

Row carried an entry about the death of Jean Guild, sister to Dr William Guild, formerly principal of King's College and 'father' of the Incorporated Trades. It ran to only three lines, but it said that Jean, 'a good sober woman', was the 'relict [widow] of David Anderson (vulgo Davie do all things)'.

Most people would have laughed at the principal's version of Anderson's nickname, for it was always said in the broad Aberdeen tongue – 'Davie dae a' thing'. David Anderson of Finzeauch, who could turn his hand to anything, got his niche in the city's history books by removing a gigantic obstruction at the entrance to the harbour. This was a huge rock called Craig Metallan. Davie got hold of a lot of empty barrels and fixed them on to the great rock at low tide. When the tide came in the rock floated to the surface and drifted out to sea.

John Row's Diary was published in instalments in *Scottish Notes and Queries*. The sixth instalment was his last, for he died of palsy [paralysis] in October 1672 at the age of seventy-four. Three years later the Diary appeared again, still carrying the title *John Row's Diary*, but now there was an introductory note which said 'Continuation by Mr Thomas Mercer, minister at Kinellar'. Thomas Mercer was the second son of John Mercer, minister of Kinellar, who was married to Lileas Row.

'From the beginning of this page', said the first entry, 'is written by me, Mr Thomas Mercer, July 21 '75.' After that came a list of John Mercer's children: four boys and five girls were named – John, Agnes, Thomas, Alexander, Christian, Isobell, Anna, Alexander and Margaret. At the end was added 'One who lieved bot 24 hours born Janr. 1674.' From then on, the 'little book' virtually became the Mercer Diary, with only a brief mention that John Row, 'leitt principall of the King's Colledge of Abd. the beginer of this book died of a palsie October 1672'.

Thomas Mercer's son John, minister of Tyrie, took over the Diary and became the 'continuator' when his father died, while *his* son John, a farmer at Kirktown of Tyrie, carried on the tradition and made entries up to 1790. The last entry in the tenth instalment of the Diary read ' John Mercer in Kirktown Tyrie, son to Mr John Mercer minister of Tyrie, died on Sabbath the 10th of January 1790 and was buried in his mother's grave in the churchyard of Tyrie. Aged seventy-three years nine months.'

Although a final line said that the Diary would be continued, nothing further appeared in *Scottish Notes and Queries*.

15

THE BIG DROP

Flurries of snow whipped over the edge of the corrie, driven by a bitter wind that snapped and gusted across the icy face of the Cairngorms. Crampons crunching on the ice, the rescuers eased the stretcher forward, tipping over the lip of the gully.

I had a sudden glimpse of sky, rock, ice and snow. Strapped to the stretcher, trussed like a chicken, I was about to be dropped down the plunging cliffs of Coire an t-Sneachda.

On the day that I became a 'casualty' with the Cairngorm Mountain Rescue team, one man died in the Glencoe hills, another was lifted off Aonach Eagach by helicopter, and a rescue team was called out when two men were reported missing on Ben Nevis.

The previous weekend ten people were missing on the hills – some on Creag Meagaidh, where the Cairngorm team had been climbing the day before I went out with them.

The 'rescue' I was on was an exercise, but it was near enough to the real

Bob Smith on the stretcher, ready for the big drop.

thing to provide a chilling taste of mountain rescue work in mid-winter.

The weather played its part. Peter Cliff, leader of the team, came out of the 'met' office at Achantoul, the team's headquarters near Aviemore, and said that the temperature was minus seven degrees. With what turned out to be a masterly piece of understatement, he added 'It's going to be windy up there.'

The exercise started with the early-morning briefing. The team's ski group, which included Sue, one of the six women members, would be dropped on Braeriach by an RAF helicopter from Lossiemouth. Four RAF aircrew would be arriving on the 'chopper' for snow training. The remainder of the team would break into groups for the exercise on Coire an t-Sneachda, the Snowy Corrie.

The truck taking us to the Cairngorm car park was driven by Ken Taylor, from Tottenham, who came to Speyside seventeen years ago and decided that this was where he wanted to live. He joined the mountain rescue team three years ago. Ken, as it turned out, was to be my 'barrow boy', the man who stuck beside the stretcher as it was lowered down Coire an t-Sneachda.

The pick-up point was across the snowfield on the approach to the corrie, where coloured smoke from a flare drifted down the valley as

Team leader Peter Cliff (left), with Graham Clark and his dog Sam.

the helicopter approached. It was there that I met Sam, who was literally straining at the leash to get going.

Sam was a golden Labrador, one of two dogs used by the Cairngorm team to sniff out climbers buried in avalanches. Graham Clark, a member of the ski patrol at the Cairngorm centre, wore a SARDA badge, insignia of the Search and Rescue Dog Association. He told me that Sam had a year's training and was still being coached.

We threw our rucksacks on to the 'chopper' window and jumped on board. I had a seat by the 'bubble' window, with Sam at my side. The engine roared, the blades beat the air, and we were away.

Below was a vast icy wasteland, capped by swollen blankets of cloud. Graham jabbed his finger to the right. Down there was Loch Einich and above it Sgor Gaoith, where on a sunlit day last year I stood and looked down on the loch. Now I had a loftier bird's-eye view.

We were over the crescent-shaped mass of Braeriach. From there, Graham told me, the ski groups would go on to Cairn Toul, down the Lairig Ghru, up on to Ben Macdhui and back by Cairngorm. They are the outriders of the mountain rescue team, moving far and fast in search and rescue operations.

The Cairngorm hills as they were on the day of the 'rescue'.

The chopper was dropping. A voice came over the earphones – 'fifty down, forty down, thirty down' ... then 'four down, two down, one down.' The pilot kept it hovering above the ground, not wanting to put the chopper on the surface.

Graham shook my hand, I gave Sam a pat, and out they spilled. Seconds later we were rising. Craning out of the 'bubble', I could see them clustered together on the summit, a tiny frozen tableau on the white canvas of Braeriach, shrinking and finally disappearing as we swung over the Garbh Choire.

Back at the pick-up point, Peter Cliff and his men were waiting for us. They clambered on board and we headed for Sneachda. This time I got out. I watched the helicopter bank above the corrie like a great dragonfly and fly south. The wind snarled across the plateau. Spindrift beat painfully against my face, like tiny needles. Peter asked me to sit on a bag to stop it blowing away and as I sat down I saw the writing on it – casualty bag.

The chopper returned with the rest of the team and preparations went ahead for the 'rescue'. Crampons were fixed, ice axes put in place, crash helmets pulled down on balaclavas, and ropes made ready. I listened uneasily as they spoke about 'dead men', but it turned out that these were metal plates which they use. The sledge was put together and ropes were slung round a huge rock on the edge of the corrie. Finally, the 'patient' was helped into the stretcher, lashed down with straps, feet braced in two loops, the casualty bag zipped up to my neck, and a crash helmet pushed on to my head.

'Well,' joked Peter, as I hovered over what suddenly seemed a nightmarish abyss, 'I think we'll go for coffee now!'

The banter was never far away. 'What happened to that chap the time the ropes broke?' Peter asked.

'My God, it was awful,' came the reply. 'He squealed like a stuck pig!'

The drop was done in three stages. Peter Cliff was on one side of the sledge, talking ceaselessly into his radio, giving instructions to the men above the ropes: 'Hold fast two, lower one.' I felt like a puppet dangling on strings.

I could see the wide white arc of the corrie on my left. Up there was where two soldiers had died the previous year. On my right was the ice and rock, and below me was the snow-choked gully down which I was being lowered nearly 1,200 feet. Ken, my barrow boy, was at the head of the stretcher, tugging, pulling, keeping it on course. His ice-crusted beard reminded me of a character from *The Last Place on Earth*. His head kept popping up to check that the patient was comfortable and that everything was all right.

Halfway down the first leg everything wasn't all right. The stretcher started to tilt, then went over on its side. Unable to move, I found myself flattened against the rock, my face touching the ice. Two or three feet away long spears of ice hung down from the rock. The stretcher was hauled back into position and I was looking at the sky again. 'What happened there?' I asked. Ken thought that a rock had thrown one of the ropes off line.

So down we went. At the end of the first leg we found John Allan perched on a ledge getting things ready for the second leg. 'Maybe it would be easier if we just cut the ropes and let you toboggan the rest of the way,' he joked.

Graham Clark and Sam with members of the team at the pick-up point.

Midget figures were moving on the snow below. Away on the left three climbers were toiling up the lower slopes of Sneachda. I could see two people staring upwards, watching the 'rescue', probably wondering who had come a cropper. There was delay when the 'talk-down' was disturbed by interference from an unknown caller. Messages crackled backwards and forwards to Glenmore and eventually the stranger went off the air.

Peter handled this and everything else with an unruffled calm. He ran his own organisation, Cairngorm Outdoor Activities, at Grantown-on-Spey, and he knew the hills like the back of his hand. He was well trusted as a leader, friendly but firm, and he believes in rigorous training. There were forty members in the team. Last year (1984) they answered an average of a call a week – four in one week – and they need £70,000 a year to keep going.

The rest of the drop was incident free. Down at the bottom two climbers passed as Ken was undoing my straps. 'I take it that was a practice,' said one, 'and not the real thing.' He got his answer when the victim rose Lazarus-like from the stretcher and heaved himself on to the snow.

Still, it felt like the real thing. The descent of Coire an t-Sneachda had taken nearly two and a half hours, and I admired the skill and dedication of those who had brought me down. But most of all I warmed to their friendliness, helpfulness and great good humour.

Before I clambered on to the Sno-cat which took me bucking and bouncing back to the ski centre, Peter Cliff gave me the only accolade I wanted. He grinned and said 'You were a good patient.'

Note: This article first appeared in the *Aberdeen Press and Journal* on 2 February 1985. Coire an t-Sneachda was described in Sir Henry Alexander's book, *The Cairngorms*, as 'the second great corrie of Cairn Gorm'. That doyen of the hills, Seton Gordon, wrote about its 'misty grandeur', with cliffs that were 'aloof and inscrutable'. Peter Cliff later gave up the leadership of the mountain rescue team and was succeeded by John Taylor, the man I saw standing on a perilous perch at the start of the second leg.

16

HIRPLETILLIM

'Daavit Drain o' Hirpletillim,
Drink never yet was brewed wad fill him;
Stout an' swack, broad breist, straucht back,
Gaed strength and swing to Hirpletillim.'

When I first read these lines from William Carnie's poem 'Hirpletillim' the name played tricks with my imagination. I thought it was a fictitious place in some far-off never-never land, a fairy-tale country where there were roses round the doors and Disney figures like Daavit Drain dancing through the woods singing happy songs.

That was a long time ago and I didn't know then that there was a Hirpletillim in Aberdeen and that I could have got to the spot, not on a magic carpet but by a No.5 tramcar to Queen's Cross.

It was to Queen's Cross that the city Fathers took Queen Victoria's statue in 1964 after it had braved the elements in St Nicholas Street for over seventy years. Here, the old Queen was set up on her plinth facing west, dreaming of her beloved Deeside. As the Aberdeen poet Alexander Scott wrote, the vogie [cheerful] queen was 'standan at Queen's Cross, her face till the fyke [bustle] of Balmoral'.

Some folk said Victoria had turned her back on the town. That may have been true, and who could blame her after years of noise and bustle in the city centre, but all around her at Queen's Cross were new streets and new buildings that had flowered during her reign, great mansion houses and garden terraces, eye-catching villas and kirks with bold spires that seemed about to rocket to the sky. The quarry on the Hill of Rubislaw had shaken itself and out of that mighty hole they had blasted a mountain of granite that was to turn this quiet corner into Nobs Hill.

W.A. Brogden, in his book *Aberdeen, an Illustrated Architectural Guide,* wrote about sober men of business leaving their plain houses in Bon-Accord Square and elsewhere to built a dream in Rubislaw Den. They weren't the only ones to build dreams about Rubislaw. In the years before the war, people from all over the town would go on a

Sunday stroll through Rubislaw just to see how the other half lived. The Lallans poet Alistair Mackie, whose grandfather, father and uncles all worked in the quarry, was taken on this Sunday pilgrimage when he was a boy.

> The granite grandery o thon road as a loun wi the family [he wrote]. How we ferlied at the grand hooses on ilkie side aa the wey up! They keekit atween the green bells o trees that the blackies jowed, the crook o their graival paths as they swung their flooers and bushes to the front door, or their trig rockeries and gressy swatches o lawn crawsteppit up to the windaes, their privet hedgeraws burst thro the jile bars o their black railings, and the trees fu o themselves blockit oot the facades or owerhung the pavement as we lytert aneth their huggert pends.

Mackie's family lived in Rubislaw Park Road, which runs from Queen's Road down to the Denburn and up past Johnston Gardens to Springfield Road. There is a row of houses on the north side. They are solid and respectable, but if you had seen them a century ago you would have recoiled at the 'foosty stink o the room wi the lie-ins', the 'nippet living rooms, the sewing machine, the press below the sink where the pots were kept among the "craal o spiders", and the sense o a human steer ye couldna read up'.

Mackie wrote about his grandfather's nieve [fist], a quarryman's nieve, red-veined and hardened by a lifetime's work in granite. 'In yon auld man's nieve grippin his luntin bouwl [pipe] I see the biggin' o the haill toun. Him and his like for mair nor a hunner years haed quarried the foonds o a city and raised it to the fower airts.'

There are no longer any hard-muscled quarrymen howkin out granite from the Rubislaw quarry, but the biggin of the toun goes on. When I was at Rubislaw Park Road I came upon a huge boarding announcing the sale of four luxury apartments. The apartments could be seen behind the board, modern, turreted, holding a flavour of the extraordinary buildings that startled the canny Aberdonians when they were built in Queen Victoria's time.

This architectural revolution took place when a group of Aberdeen businessmen formed the City of Aberdeen Land Association with the aim of buying up land and feuing it out or reselling it on smaller lots for development. In that first year they bought Fountainhall, Rubislaw and Morningfield, followed by Torry and Craiginches across the Dee. It cost £130,000, but the Torry quines got their hooses as well as the posh folk across the water.

I set out to find out how that 'granite grandery' had fared over the century that had gone. Cuthbert Graham, with whom I worked on the old *Weekly Journal* just after the war, wrote about the road by Alford Place and Albyn Place to Queen's Road – the old Alford coach road, now an area of stately terraces fronted by lawns and flower-beds and lined with great trees. 'This was the nineteenth-century design for gracious living,' he said.

When I set off from Queen's Cross I thought of what Alistair Mackie had said about the road ahead. 'Oh the lang straucht o Queen's Road!' As he wandered around the leafy lawns and trim streets he thought he was seeing the 'deid hooses of the livin', or was't the livin' hooses o the deid'. Nobody was ever at the windows, he said, 'naebody on the lawns, naebody we ever kent bade in them'. His father said they were fishermen's hooses, or quarrymaisters'.

In fact, everybody who was anybody, or wanted to be somebody, had clawed their way into the city's burgeoning West End. It was appropriate that the first house built west of Albyn Place in 1864 was by an accountant, Robert Fletcher. It was said to be the largest house in Aberdeen, but it was taken over by a convent.

The race was on. Fields and estates and roads were gobbled up by the house hunters: bankers, bakers, shipmasters, shareholders, newspaper editors (Sir Henry Alexander and William Watt, both of the *Free Press*), ministers, and advocates. Among the legal men was Lachlan Mackinnon, a lawyer of considerable repute, who lived at No.8 Queen's Road. It had little resemblance to the Queen's Road of today.

Back from the road was the dwelling house and other farm buildings of Rubislaw Farm. Stones from the farm were used to build No.8. Nearby was a toll house and opposite it was a white-washed, one-storeyed range of low buildings with a two-storeyed house in the middle where Alexander Coutts operated a grocer's shop. Lachlan Mackinon described Coutts as 'an old gentleman who served his customers personally in a white apron and velvet smoking cap'.

While new mansions mushroomed in Rubislaw, time was running out for a building that had dominated the area for centuries – the old

Rubislaw House, home of the Skenes of Rubislaw. This is how Lawyer Mackinon saw it before its demolition in 1886.

> The old house of Rubislaw (with courtyard in front) stood west of the toll house. The Skene coat-of-arms, much mutilated by stone throwers, showed in a panel above the main door, to which there was access by a flight of stone steps with iron railings. The house was in bad order, and was used as a tenement dwelling for workers. A shattered corner of the old garden was still standing north-west of the house and the line of the original approach avenue was indicated by the trees that bordered a narrow road to the south.

The house was built by Arthur Forbes in 1675. The main south-facing block was a rectangular, three-storey building. The estate was bought by Sir George Skene of Fintray in 1687. He had his coat-of-arms placed in a panel above the entrance, and he added two flanking wings to the house. John Morgan, the Aberdeen master builder, wanted to preserve Old Rubislaw House, or part of it. He planned to save the original walls, leaving the exterior unchanged, but it stood in the way of straightening Queen's Road and the plan was dropped. Instead, a new house was built almost on the site. It was designed by the architect John Pirie, of Pirie & Clyne, and it was called Pirie's masterpiece.

The word 'bizarre' has been frequently used in comments on the house. Alec Keith, in his *A Thousand Years of Aberdeen*, described it as 'that amazing baroque edifice No.50 Queen's Road', and more recently Ronald MacInnes in *The Aberdeen Guide* said it was 'a most bizarre masterpiece of baronial forms crushed together in one composition'.

It seemed to me that the new House of Rubislaw, as Morgan called it, almost belonged to the fairy-tale world of Hirpletillim. It stands apart from the other buildings. In this confusion of towers and turrets and other architectural whimsies it is different, it is bizarre, and yet it has a certain dignity about it. MacInnes wasn't far off the mark when he said it was 'the best house of Aberdeen's nineteenth-century expansion'.

There was a house in Rubislaw Den North that seemed to carry experimental building to excess. It was built four years before Morgan's mansion. Bill Brogden called it 'the spooky Rubislawden House', adding that 'the architect (if any) was thankfully unknown'. It was, he said, 'all bays, towers, turrets and pointed windows but somehow doesn't quite make it to Transylvania'.

Happily, No.50 Queen's Road stands as a magnificent tribute to Aberdeen's master mason, John Morgan. This remarkable man was born on a small holding at Craighall, Kennethmont in 1844 and had a poor education. He started work as an apprentice with his uncle, Adam Mitchell, a builder, in 1862, and fifty years later took control of the firm. He built up an impressive list of major projects, including

John Morgan's masterpiece on Queen's Road.

the laying out of Union Terrace gardens, the building of the public library, the creation of the city's fish market, and the building of the plinth for William Wallace's statue.

A plague to John Morgan and above it a sundial on the house he built.

The gaps in his education he filled by his own endeavours. He was an admirer of John Ruskin, the English author and art critic, and he was intensely interested in the Pre-Raphaelite period. In his Queen's Road home he installed three stained-glass windows – Faith, Hope and Charity. From a lane at the back of his house you can see the band of windows that look into the library he had made to house his book collection – four and a half thousand of them!

The lane is called Spademill Lane and it branches off Spademill Road, which runs alongside the eighteenth-century toll house, now a restaurant and shop. These once-dusty byways, now tarred and bedaubed with double yellow lines, have uncomely names, but they recall an interesting period in Rubislaw's history.

The name Spademill comes from the manufacture of wooden spades used for turning barley in the nearby Glenburnie whisky distillery, which closed in 1857. Spademill Road and Spademill Lane were part of an old cross-country route leading to the Stocket and the Old Skene Road. But, for me, Spademill had another interest – it was the gateway to Hirpletillim. As I walked along the tree-lined track I could see a house facing me on Rubislaw Den South. It was No.16, and it was said that it was on this site that Hirpletillim had once stood.

Not much has been written about Hirpletillim, and not all of it has been accurate. It has been called a croft, a hamlet, a house, even two rows of houses, but the picture above doesn't really settle the argument. Alec Keith said that 'the central part of that impressive thoroughfare (Rubislaw Den South) was the croft of Hirpletillim, the chief house of which coincided fairly nearly with the site of No. 6'.

Fenton Wyness wrote about 'the fascinating hamlet of Hirpletillim, a charming collection of red-tiled cottages which survived until 1879'.

Hirpletillim was there as far back as the eighteenth century. I discovered this when I came upon an advertisement in the *Aberdeen Daily Journal* regarding the letting of 'Kingswood Farm at Hirpletillum [sic] in August 1796' and another in 1797. The first was 'to let the ground and house lately occupied by William Reid situated on the north side of the Den of Rubislaw, that piece of ground called the Kingswood'. The tenant would have the right to the trees but would be obliged to remove them and trench the ground within a limited time.

The second advertisement was for the let of 'the farm of

Hirpletillum presently possessed by Robert McIntyre with the piece of barren ground betwixt Hirpletillum and the Dee, and a park near Hirpletillum with the dwelling house, barn and bleach green lately possessed by William Wallace'. A dwelling house and a large fruit garden, lately occupied by James Birnie, were also mentioned in the advertisement. 'Proposals in writing,' it said, 'may be given in to the proprietor at his lodgings in Mrs Stewart's opposite to Adam's Hotel.'

So, if Fenton Wyness was correct in saying that the 'hamlet' of Hirpletillim survived until 1879, a new Hirpletillim was waiting to rise from its ashes. Robert Anderson, editor of the *Free Press,* wrote in his book *Aberdeen in Bygone Days* in 1910 that a Mr James Clyne had built one of the first houses in the new street (Rubislaw Den South). That house is now No.24. The date Anderson gave was '1879 or thereabouts'. 'He called it Hirpletillim,' wrote Anderson, 'but the name does

Spademill Road.
The house at the end of it was said to be the site of Hirpletillim.

not seem to be now used.'

James Clyne, who may have been related to Arthur Clyne, of the Pirie & Clyne partnership, obviously had some emotional reaction to Hirpletillim. Perhaps he was sad at the thought of this old hamlet being wiped out to make way for the foibles of Victorian architects. Whatever the uncertainties about Hirpletillim's age and appearance, there was little doubt that it was an idyllic spot.

Anderson, who could find little to say about Hirpletillim because 'it has virtually no history', nevertheless described it as 'a picturesque group of old-fashioned, red-tiled structures, smothered in flowers and evergreens'. He was glad the name Hirpletillim had been preserved, not by Mr Clyne but by 'a very happy poem' written by William Carnie in 1893.

I have often wondered if Carnie's poem was about the real Hirpletillim, or a fictitious one. If it was the real thing then Hirpletillim was a farm and not a group of houses or a cottage for Carnie wrote about 'things gaun in byre and barn' and being 'up wi' the lark – fae morn to dark'. It is interesting that he adopted the old custom of calling the farmer, not by his own name but by the name of his farm, as seen in his argument with the laird, 'Wi' fear nae soul micht try instil him, Even Ury's laird, wi' feint and gaird, Was scarce a match for Hirpletillim.'

But all these questions and mysteries are lost now, pushed into the past by the 'granite grandery' that has taken over Rubislaw. This is how William Carnie ended his poem,

> Here's nae sic men a-makin' noo
> As ane I kent near Robslaw quarries;
> His een are closed, cauld, cauld his broo,
> He's deen wi' a' life's cares and sharries [quarrels].
> Daavit Drain o' Hirpletillim,
> What mortal born could e'er ill-will him?
> But noo he's gane – and 'neath yon stane
> Nae bode can wauken Hirpletillim.

It may be that some day someone walking about the trig rockeries and crawsteppit lawns in Rubislaw will find a stane buried in the undergrowth and will wonder at the inscription on it, 'Daavit Drain o' Hirpletillim, What mortal born could e'er ill-will him?'

17

BUFFALO BILL

It began on a Saturday morning in late August 1904. That day, all roads led to Kittybrewster, and it seemed as if the whole population of Aberdeen was determined to get there. From eleven o'clock, according to the *Aberdeen Journal*, a 'constantly-moving stream of humanity, ever increasing in number, was flowing towards Kittybrewster'.

More than thirty tramcars were running on the Woodside route, and every empty tram arriving back at Queen Victoria's statue in St Nicholas Street was besieged by the waiting crowd. The old call 'Meet you at the Queen!' had become farcical.

So what was it that stirred the phlegmatic Aberdonians to such a frenzy? Well, the Wild West had arrived. 'Buffalo Bill' Cody and his Congress of Rough Riders were in town as part of a final farewell trip around Britain. They were visiting 'the Principal Cities and Greater Railway Centres only.' Posters advertised the thrills that lay in store for those eager masses. It would be 'an Exhibition of Marvellous Merit, presented Twice Daily rain or shine, an exhibition that Teaches but does not Imitate'. There would be 500 horses and 800 people taking part.

The tramcars that clattered up George Street were utterly inadequate. Streets running on to George Street were crowded with people hoping to get on to the trams, but every vehicle was loaded up at the starting point. The situation was made worse by the influx of country people. Never, it was reported, had so many special trains run into Aberdeen. The show was going on to Fraserburgh and Peterhead after Aberdeen, but canny farmers and the like couldn't resist the cheap fares offered by the railway company.

By twelve o'clock a huge multitude had gathered at Kittybrewster and the ticket boxes were besieged when they were opened at 12.30. Half an hour before the show started there were 10,000–12,000 present, and still the stream flowed into the enclosure. By two o'clock another thousand had joined the audience – 13,000 country folk and toonsers sitting on the edge of their seats waiting to greet Colonel W.F. Cody and his army of Wild West entertainers.

Buffalo Bill didn't let them down. The show wasn't confined to cowboys and Indians. There were Mexican vaqueros, Bedouin Arabs, South American gauchos, Cuban patriots and imperial Japanese troops. There was also an intrepid cowboy who did a daredevil leap through space – not on a horse but on a bicycle. There was even a corps from the United States Life Savers demonstrating the methods employed with the breeches buoy.

The audience thrilled to Indian war dances, a stagecoach hold-up, an attack on an emigrant train, and the great battles of the West – the Battle of the Little Big Horn and Custer's Last Stand. The greatest ovation was for Colonel Cody, taking his place 'at the head of his fearless riders from all lands'. The *Aberdeen Journal* reported on 'the marvellous display of horsemanship, especially by the Cossacks and cowboys' and on the 'great leap by the cowboy cyclist'.

A representative of the *Aberdeen Journal* was invited to become one of the passengers in the 'Deadwood' coach which was attacked by Indians.

> Drawn at a rapid rate by a spanking team of six [the *Journal* man reported], the coach bounds along and gives one such a shaking up as to prompt the thought that there is certainly more than one kind of 'rough riding', while the experience of being surrounded by a large troop of mounted Indians – in all the glory of their war paint – keeping up a perfect fusillade with their firearms while many of them actually peer in at the windows of the coach, which might make most people a little nervous for the moment.

By four o'clock the performance was over, but it was followed by a concert, and people began to drift to the sideshows. The Midget – 'a little marvel of humanity' – was a huge success, but the giant and other attractions also did their bit. Business was 'unexceptionally good'.

The great crowds that gathered at Kittybrewster kept the police on their toes. 'In the work of protecting the public from the operations of any of the "light-fingered gentry",' reported the *Journal,* 'the city's police had the valuable assistance of Mr C. Murphy, one of the assistant superintendents of Pinkerton's National Detective Agency, New York.' Pinkerton's man, it seemed, had knowledge 'of many of the most celebrated thieves of the world'. It paid off – not a single loss was reported.

Buffalo Bill and his team drew in 74,000 people in their three days at 'Kitty'. That was 2,000 more than Dundee was able to pull in, which no doubt delighted the Aberdeen organisers. When the final evening show was taking place on Saturday evening, three special trains at Kittybrewster station were standing by to move the whole show to Peterhead. In less than three hours after the performance closed, the first train was on its way. The second left half an hour later and the third at twenty-five minutes past one. In all, there were sixty-five vehicles on the three trains.

Canny Buchan went daft over Buffalo Bill and his Wild West troupe. 'Peterhead regarded it as a nine-day wonder the like of which they would never see again,' the *Peterhead Sentinel* commented. The nine-day wonder lasted only one day in the Blue Toon, but the *Sentinel* applauded it as 'a red-letter day in the annals of sensational and spectacular entertainment'.

There were two performances, drawing 21,000 spectators. But on top of the twenty-three items on the programme, the Peterhead folk enjoyed a free 'show' on the streets of the town. The *Sentinel* told of Cossacks in turbans and vaqueros with curly-brimmed hats, cowboys with shirts and ties that did not seem to call for much washing. They walked jauntily along the pavements, not neglecting the lasses, and the streets were transformed by the sight of fierce-looking Indians stamping past shops and houses followed by fans from seven to seventy. It was a change from the familiar sight of ferm loons and fishers. This was a colourful, exciting, unbelievable spectacle – Buffalo Bill and his Rough Riders of the World had arrived in Buchan with a bang!

The Broch was the next stop. The same enormous 'flitting' took place to get the show on the road on Tuesday, 30 August. Forty-nine special wagons were laid on for the trip to Fraserburgh, the tents were hauled up and the seats were put in place. It was on with the show. They seemed to come from all over Buchan, from Inverallochy, Cairnbulg and St Combs, and from Lonmay, Maud and Strichen, and horse-drawn conveyances carried sightseers from New Aberdour, Rosehearty, Cumineston and New Byth.

Colonel W.F. Cody was a skilled publicist. Just after eleven o'clock in the morning he rode down the South Pier at the head of a cavalcade of Red Indians. They had their photographs taken, and anyone who saw them back in the Wild West must have wondered at seeing a background of the masts of herring drifters. The Indians dismounted and walked to the rocks below Kinnaird Head, where more photographs were taken. After that, they went on a tour of the Kinnaird Head Preserve Works. They each left with a souvenir – a tin of Maconnochie's canned herring!

There were 19,000 spectators at the Fraserburgh performances. The local paper, the *Herald,* dug up some interesting information about the food needed for the visitors from the Wild West. The daily cost for keeping the show on the road was £700, mostly for 600 loaves, 25 hundredweight of meat, 880 pounds of potatoes, 1,400 pounds of other vegetables, 600 bushes of oats, 6 tons of straw and 6 tons of hay. It all added up to regular meals for 800 people and 500 horses.

The next stop for the show was Huntly, a one-day stand in which one of the Indians called Little Bear was left in the local hospital suffering from a festered foot. He was out and about again the following Sunday, when he donned his full Indian costume and war paint and attended the forenoon service in the Roman Catholic Church. It was later reported that Little Bear was 'fit to rejoin his wigwam in Perth'.

18

THE MONKEY HOUSE

They called it the Monkey House – a strange name for one of Aberdeen's finest granite buildings. It looks out on the roar and rush of the city at the junction of Union Street and Union Terrace. It has been there for over a century, its dignified, imposing frontage adding lustre to the glory of granite. It was designed by the architect A. Marshall Mackenzie and it has been described as 'superb' and 'undeniably splendid'. Built in 1885 for the Northern Assurance Company, it later became the Commercial Union Insurance building, but it has always been known as the Monkey House.

The main feature of the building is its Doric porch, whose pillars have enticed generations of Aberdonians into the doorway for a 'date' or for shelter. You could wait there for a tram on a rainy day and then make a run for it. It was a place where boy met girl, where

The Monkey House, where generations of Aberdonians met in the pillared doorway for a 'date' or shelter.

relationships were formed that led to a walk down the aisle, and where a familiar phrase was born, 'Meet you at the Monkey House.'

I remember how in those pre-war days they crowded into the entrance, out of the rain, with everyone peering out behind the pillars like monkeys in a cage. That was how it got its nickname, and not because of 'monkey business' at the Mat, as one writer, Ranald MacInnes, suggested in his book *Aberdeen Guide*. The Mat was a stretch of Union Street where you promenaded on a Sunday night in the hope of finding a 'date', a ritual that has long since gone.

Farther down Union Street to the east a rival call might have been heard, 'Meet you at the Queen.' That was before the St Nicholas Centre cut off George Street from the heart of the city, back in the days when tramcars came bumping and rattling down George Street to disgorge their passengers at Queen Victoria's statue. It stood at the south-east corner off St Nicholas Street for seventy years and in 1964 was moved to Queen's Cross, where she could gaze longingly towards Balmoral.

In 1962, Aberdeen's librarian, Marcus Milne, wrote about the Queen and the Monkey House and about 'walking the Mat'. The headline to his article in the *Press and Journal* read 'We walked the Mat and met the Queen (never the Monkey House).'

The Monkey House.

'Union Street has been the "Mecca" for young people since it was laid out in 1800,' he wrote. 'When I was young we walked the "Mat" and usually met at the Queen. I don't know what name is given to Union Street today, but I hear young people speak of meeting at the "Monkey House". Strange that so august a building should be so named.'

The Mat was generally regarded as the south side of Union Street from Bridge Street to Holburn Junction. On Sunday nights it drew a host of teenagers who paraded up and down the pavement or stood in shadowy shop doors and watched the passing 'talent'. Mostly, it was innocent fun, but times have changed. The 'Mat' has become a place where police keep an eye open for drugs, mugging and violence.

The north side of Union Street was never part of the Mat, although it had its own attractions. It was on that side in pre-war days that you went to Babs Wilson's dancing class to learn how to do the foxtrot – 'slow, slow, quick, quick, slow', urged Babs – and after it you sat among the rafters and knocked back soft drinks. Later, you graduated to the Palais in Diamond Street, where Mr Bromberg ruled the roost, and where you knocked back a stronger brew.

When I was standing in the doorway of the Monkey House I thought of how this busy junction was, and probably still is, the pulse of the city. There was a touch of grandeur about it in the old days. At the top of Bridge Street was George Pegler's fruit shop, whose mouth-watering fruit was said to be 'the cheapest in the market'. Across Bridge Street, next to the Union Bridge, was the elegant Palace Hotel, built in 1874 and burned down in October 1941, while facing it across the street was the massive statue of King Edward VII. The statue got a mixed reception from writers. Ranald MacInnes wrote about 'the wonderfully restored and gilded statue of Edward VII', while Lewis Grassic Gibbon thought it 'merely vulgar' and the poet Alistair Mackie dismissed the King as 'that fat clort'.

To keep the history books right they should have plumped down another statue of the first man over the Union Bridge. He was 'a gentleman on horseback' who clip-clopped his way into the pages of the *Aberdeen Journal* by riding over the bridge three months before it was officially opened. It turned out that he was given special permission to do this, but as far as I know there is no record of who he was – or why he did it. I have a picture in my mind of this 'gentleman on horseback' disappearing into the distance with a smug smile on his face, wondering how he got away with it.

They flung up statues along Union Terrace – the Valhalla of the famous, they called it – but there is no statue to a man who was famous in his own way, for he was known to thousands of Aberdonians. He was the legendary news vender Patsy Gallacher, who had his news stand outside the Monkey House. Everybody knew Patsy; I could swear that the old king on his pedestal gave him a wink now and again. Being a bit of a ladies' man, Edward might have been interested in one of Patsy's sidelines He was said to augment his income by supplying regular customers with condoms, or French letters as they were called in those innocent days. It was all done very discreetly; he slipped the condom between the pages of the paper I edited, the *Evening Express.*

The Monkey House has been a silent witness to all these goings on. If Marcus Milne thought it strange that Marshall Mackenzie's masterpiece should be given such a name, he would find it a good deal stranger now, for the insurance building has become a restaurant, and on each side of the doorway, in large letters, are the words 'The Monkey House'. What's more, there are monkeys watching you from a window, not real-life monkeys, but very artistic ones.

A monkey in the window of the Monkey House.

The Commercial Union building was converted into a restaurant and bar by Mike Wilson and Billy Cowe, of a company called the Epic Group. Both Mike, the owner of the restaurant, and Billy were originally connected with the fishing industry. 'Mike was in the buying side,' said Billy, 'and I was in the catching side.' A Fraserburgh man, he was a fisherman for fifteen years. Now they are 'casting their net' in the property market. They had sold a hotel in Skye when I met Billy and had bought the Haughton Arms Hotel in Alford. Their ultimate aim is to set up a chain of Scottish hotels.

It was Billy who showed me round the Monkey House, through a maze of corridors, upstairs and downstairs, past reminders of the insurance days: for instance, a big heavy door into the old safe, now carrying a notice saying 'This sink for pot wash only', and heavy wooden slatted blinds on the windows that no one knew about. It is thought they were made for the wartime blackout. Then there was the 'secret' passage which Billy found behind one of the walls – a series of arches and alcoves running under Union Street, like a setting from the *The Third Man* film. Billy didn't know if you could do an Orson Welles and climb out of the passage into Union Street.

The most interesting 'find' in the building was a pair of scrolls discovered in a cellar of the bar. They were held in two long metal tubes stamped with the words 'Property of Aberdeen and District Museum'. Billy unrolled one of the scrolls, which seemed to be an insurance policy for the building. It was fifteen feet long, and filled with tiny handwritten script. There were references to the 'Bon-Accord Life Assurance, guaranteed revisionary', and to the 'North of Scotland Life and Fire contracts'. We laid the scroll on the floor, stretching it out like an enormous carpet, covered with line after line of insurance details. I wondered who had undertaken this mammoth task and why it had been done that way. But to find the answer I would have had to go back more than a century and a half. The date on the scroll was 1836.

There are four storeys and a basement in the Monkey House. The plan is to use the upper floors for hotel accommodation at some date in the future, perhaps in a couple of years. The need for a good Scottish-type hotel in Aberdeen is very much in Billy's mind. Edinburgh had them, he said, and Glasgow, but not Aberdeen. If that happens it would fill the gap left when the old Palace Hotel was burned down more than sixty years ago. The Monkey House had considerable elegance as an insurance building and none of it has been lost by conversion to a restaurant. It is a Grade A listed building and the beautiful woodwork has been retained.

Whether or not the name would remain is another matter. There have already been moves to change the 'Monkey House' signs over the door and to have the monkeys removed from the windows. The argument, says Billy, is that they are not in line with what an old building ought to be. I hope that the name is retained in some form, for it is as much a part of the city's tradition as Robbie Burns and his daisy.

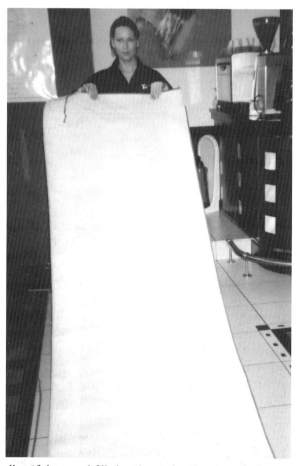

This scroll, 15ft long and filled with tiny handwritten script, was found in the cellar of the bar. It was dated 1836.

19

AULD JEANNIE GELLAN

The old tracks thread their way south from Kemnay, pushing on to farms with curious names like Tillybin and Leschangie, Tappies and Todfold. I had seen on a map the mosses that had put their black fingers across this countryside, among them Bandshed Moss, Firley Moss and Lauchintilly Moss. The name Bandshed meant a ridge dividing two mosses, *band* being the top or summit, *shed* a portion of land. Firley was also given as Fairley, which was how it was pronounced. As for Lauchintilly, the Gaelic for it was *lachduinn tulaidh* [grey hillock].

Jeannie Gellan's gravestone in Kemnay churchyard.

But I was hurrying away from grey hillocks and dark mosses. I was looking for a place with a bonnier, brighter face, a 'wee cot-hame' called Sunnybrae, where a lass called Jeannie Gellan had settled with her new husband, Jamie Laing, in the early years of the nineteenth century. To the young couple this lonely spot was 'clad in the glamour o' young love's dreams'. It was 'beauty and pleasure galore'. They thought it was like paradise.

I first read about Jeannie Gellan in an old copy of *Scottish Notes and Queries*. It was dated 1889 and it carried a piece on the longevity of Aberdonians, mentioning people like Peter Hatt, who died in 1816 aged 102, and a nameless woman who had 'lived to fully 100 and never required spectacles'. But one person held my attention more than the others, for she was singled out from the rest of them. She was described as 'an old woman named Jeanie Gallen, who died at the age of ninety'.

The contributor of this tale of longevity pointed out that Dr Andrew Edgar, author of *Old Church Life in Scotland,* had said that the erection of tombstones was a comparatively modern custom, and only for distinguished individuals. 'Jeanie', he went on, 'has been fortunate enough to get a handsome tombstone erected to her memory, with her last words engraved upon it.' Her last words were 'It maiters na whaure we lie doon if we sleep in the hope o' a glorious risin'.'

There was also a poem, entitled 'Auld Jeanie's Death-bed', written by an unnamed author whose initials were W.C. The poem ran to twenty-five stanzas and, it was said, 'embodied the many superstitions in which Jeannie was a devout believer'. It turned out that the mysterious W.C. was the Aberdeen poet, William Cadenhead, who had also paid for the handsome stone. Oddly enough, one of Cadenhead's early poems was set in Kemnay. It was called 'The Devil's Stane' and it told how Auld Nick had thrown a great stone at the kirk yard where Auld Jeannie was buried. The prayers of a priest 'turned the murderous rock aside' and it 'lichted doon' in a nearby field.

Cadenhead was born in the Poynernook area of Aberdeen in 1819. He would have been fifty-nine when Jeannie died. He became overseer in the yarn-sorting department of Broadford Works, and there seems nothing to connect him to Kemnay apart from his 'Devil's Stane' poem. How he came to know Jeannie I do not know, but he obviously had a close relationship with her. This is clearly shown in

'Auld Jeannie's Death-bed'. It is Cadenhead who writes the lines, but it is Jeannie who speaks them, 'O lift me up i' the bed awee', she says, 'for I hinna lang to be here.'

She looks back on the time when she and her husband Jamie first came to Sunnybrae, 'O, weel do I min' when Jamie first sought me here to this wee cot-hame; 'Twas the outcome fain, an' the honest birst. O' a strong an' a true-love flame.'

She tells how she had 'a sair wrastle a' my life', how Jamie had little when they were married and she had less, and how they were happy at Sunnybrae; they had 'rowan and red thread' above their door to ward off evil spells. Sadly, it wasn't enough to keep away the ill luck that changed their lives, 'Alack! Our sorrows grew fast an' thick; oor beasts dwin'd ane by ane; waste away an' Jamie himsel' at length grew sick an' dee'd, an' maist left me alane.'

When I went south in search of Sunnybrae I was seeing the land through Auld Jeannie's eyes, 'O, sweet were the scents as in summer I fared by the beauties o' Green Kirtle Road.' This was a long straight road stretching away to Leschangie. It is now known as Wellbush. 'Wheesht!' she cried. 'I hear you a strummin' amang the knowes [knolls] out o'er Lochshangie shaw.' The name Lochshangie (or Leschangie) means a wooded ridge with farms. The word 'shaw' means flat ground at the bottom of a hill.

The first road I took ended up at Todfold. I had been told that Sunnybrae had lain south of it. The farmhouse here is smart and modern, the approach to it well designed. It was aeons away from the cottar house that would have been there when the Earl of Kintore's tenants lived in it. Lindsay Dewar and his wife Marion have been there for forty years. The name Todfold comes from tod [fox], and Lindsay told me that foxes could still be seen prowling about the farms.

I thought that with forty years behind them they must know something about Sunnybrae, but they didn't, although Marion had heard the name. She pointed out woodlands to the west where she thought it might have been. I had to drive back into Kemnay, go round the recreation park and follow a track beyond it. I was going into Leschangie country again – an area I wrote about three years ago when I was writing a book about walks around Aberdeen.

Ten years ago that track took me over Leschangie Hill to the

Leschangie quarries. At one of the major quarries, the long arc of its granite face covered a large part of the hill. Neat blocks of pink-grey granite stood on the edge of it. It was bare, bleak and deserted, yet it was from Leschangie Hill that they blasted granite that was said to be of a much finer quality than the famous Kemnay granite.

If Lady Luck had played her cards differently Leschangie granite might have become famous and Kemnay granite would have slipped into the background. What decided it was the Alford Valley Railway's plan to take the rail route on a curve round Tom's Forest and past the quarries on Paradise Hill to Kemnay. For Leschangie, as I wrote at the time, it was Paradise Lost.

Lauchintilly was another name that struck chords with me. It is a name that rubs shoulders with Leschangie to the south of Todfold. When I was exploring the Lyne of Skene area for my book *The Road to Maggieknockater* I met Bill Anderson, who farmed at Lauchintilly and I met his Uncle Jimmy, a spry old-timer in his nineties, who lived with his wife Betty at a cottar house called Scrapehard, a name that the factor changed to Nether Lauchintilly.

Leschangie … Lauchintilly … neither of them brought me nearer to Sunnybrae, although I had a feeling it had been somewhere there. But there was no trace of the wee cottar-hame, not a sign, not a stone, to show that it had ever been there. I decided to abandon my search and head for the kirk yard at Kemnay, where the Devil had thrown his rock and where Auld Jeannie Gellan's story ended.

She was a pious woman. The Lord, she said, had 'aye sweetened my cup'. She died at Sunnybrae on 5 May 1878 at the age of ninety-two. Part of William Cadenhead's poem tells how she faced death. These are the verses:

> Aye! That's the faith that has cheer'd my life,
> An' will charm tae the hour I dee –
> An' sick o' the pain an' the trouble an' strife,
> I carena how soon that may be!

> But I tak' you boun', when I wear awa',
> That ye'll see me tae'en richt about,
> An' at kistin', an' lake, 'mang my neighbours a',
> I'll be decent an' fairly laid out.

My graif-claiths ye'll get them faul'd up i' the ark,
    Weel wivin an' fair bleach'd;
The weavin' was honest customer-wark,
    The yarn was my maiden-spinnin'.

An' ye'll see me laid safely aneath the heap –
    I' the spot o' oor ain folks chisin;
Tho' it maiters na whaure we lie doon, if we sleep
    In the hope o' a glorious risin'.

Jeannie hoped she would be 'fairly laid out for the kistin'. A kistin',
or kisting, was the laying of a corpse in its coffin on the night before
the funeral, when there were accompanying ceremonies and entertainment. Her graif-claiths [grave clothes] were folded up in the ark
[large chest]. The spot where she was buried was, as the poem said, of

Kemnay Parish Church, where Auld Jeannie Gellan was buried. The 'handsome
stone', as it was described, was a small memorial little more than three feet
high. It is seen in the front of the picture, between two large gravestones.

103

her own folks choosing, in a corner of the kirk yard at Kemnay parish church.

The church has been described as 'plain and not very old', but it was built on an ancient site. The burial vault of the Burnetts of Kemnay, dating back to 1720, stands against the wall of the church. Cadenhead wrote about how Jeannie would sit in the kirk and watch the sunbeams streaming in at the 'winnock', but there are no sunbeams lighting up the old kirk yard, with its gloomy flat grave-stones and fading epitaphs. It is there that Auld Jeannie Gellan is buried.

There are four tombstones for the Laing family. Two of the stones carry the names of Laings and their relatives, while the face of a third has completely worn away, although it is known to mark the grave of a Laing. Some had links with Cluny Castle, among them Robert Laing, a coachman, who was at the castle stables for twenty years.

Then there is Jeannie Gellan's stone, the 'handsome stone' paid for by William Cadenhead. It is, in fact, a sad sight, a tawdry memorial little more than three feet high, its surface scoured by wind and rain, its letters fading. It is anything but handsome, but it may have seemed so when it was first placed there. Beneath it lie Jeannie and her beloved Jamie, who, as the poem says, were drawn together by 'a strong and true-love flame'.

20

THE LENABO SOOS

There is a land, a treeless land,
where all the bravest go.
It raineth every day and night,
We call it Lenabo!

They called them the Lenabo soos because that's what airships
looked like in the First World War, flying pigs, 'soos' [sows] in the
local dialect, great, bulbous machines that rose from the 'treeless land'
and went off to guard our shipping lanes. Their airship base was at
Lenabo, a bare, boggy corner of Buchan that seemed locked away
from the outside world.

It was Britain's most northerly airship station, and the airmen
who came to it from faraway places were not entranced with what
they found. They said it had risen from a primeval bog. Bogs, bogs,
bogs ... they were everywhere. It was poetic justice that one of the
first farms to be swept away by the development was Bogend. When
a poetry competition was held on the station the prize-winning
verse was this,

There once was a Station, you see,
Not far from the mouth of the Dee,
It consisted of bogs,
Squalls, tempests and fogs,
A Longside with mists from the sea.

The newcomers, as well as being soured by the north-east weather,
thought little of its culture, or its scenery. Buchan, they said, couldn't
claim any distinction in the domain of artistic achievement.

The uninspiring character of the scenery may have contributed to
deaden the aspirations of a people who apparently have few local
songs or ballads such as witness to fine old traditions in the south.
Such lyrics as there are appear to be uncouth rhymes very redolent of
bucolic wit and rustic idiom, and are concerned chiefly with the
humour of the farmyard.

Gavin Greig, the great collector of north-east ballads, who died in 1914, would have thought little of that comment.

The decision to equip the Royal Naval Air Service with submarine-searching airships was taken in 1915. Three airships were stationed at Scapa Flow but they were unable to cope with the strong winds around Orkney and all three were lost at sea. The Scapa site was abandoned and work started on a number of new stations farther south on the mainland. Lenabo was one of them.

Lenabo began to take shape in the early months of 1915. Living quarters, gasworks, cinema, canteen, engineering shop, hangars – they mushroomed on the peaty Buchan spoil with incredible speed. Crofts were swallowed up and an army of navvies worked through the night by the light of napalm flares. William Tawse & Sons, Aberdeen, were given the job of building the station and the first thing they did was erect a small village of huts for their men. Tawsetown was born. Instead of old farm names like Torhendry and Backhill there were the Tawse huts, the Auchtydore huts, the Braeside huts and the Lenabo huts.

A memorial marking the site of the Lenabo airship station. A plaque on the memorial tells the story of the Lenabo 'soos'.

Although the station was ready by the autumn of 1915, it was 1916 before it became fully operational. The RNAS operated three classes of airship from Lenabo: a scouting ship, the SS *Zero*, with a crew of three, a flight duration of twelve hours and a range of 200 miles; a Coastal with a crew of five and a range of over 500 miles; and a North Sea class ship with a crew of ten and an extreme range of 2,000 miles.

The air gunner acted as look-out and was also the cook, frying or stewing food heated by exhaust gases from the engines. Capt P.E. (Eric) Maitland, who eventually rose to the rank of Air Vice-Marshal, once claimed to be the first man to cook eggs and bacon in the air, but he never actually tasted them. He opened the cut-out from the exhaust too wide and eggs and bacon disappeared into the propeller.

What the canny Buchan folk thought about it all is anybody's guess. They must have watched uneasily as great squads of men descended on Lenabo to tear it apart and build an airship station. They would have seen the dirigibles [airships], with their grey fat bellies, lurching over their fields, ropes dangling from them, brushing

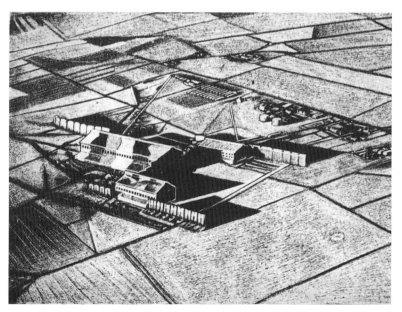

A plan of the Lenabo air station.

trees and farm steadings. When an airship was landing it took a hundred ratings to grasp the guy ropes and hold the ship down. It was a hazardous business. A sudden gust of wind could swing it against a building and men could be thrown about, dragged, as one pilot put it, 'like terriers with a platoon of rats'.

One of the first airships to go into action from Lenabo was *NS3*, under Flight-Commander J.S. Wheelwright, with Capt. Maitland as second pilot. In May 1918 oil was spotted rising from the sea off Montrose and *NS3* dropped 3 230-pound bombs in the area. A destroyer followed up by dropping depth charges on the airship's bomb marks and oil and wreckage were seen spewing up on the surface. Later, it turned out that they had bombed the wreck of a British submarine lost in the North Sea earlier in the year.

In June of that year the *NS3* was hit by a gale. It dropped, hit the water and had its engines ripped off. Capt. Maitland described how, after dropping into the water, he climbed on to the rigid flat part of the envelope and found the captain and coxswain there. When dawn broke, a destroyer took some of the crew off, but two engineers, the coxswain, air gunner and wireless operator were lost.

The Lenabo soos acted as escorts to convoys of as many as forty ships. From the 'gasbags' they could see the merchantmen pushing ahead in three columns, under the watchful eye of two destroyers. When the fliers had to endure a six- or seven-hour stint, chocolate and iron-hard biscuits were served in the open cockpits of the smaller airships. Crews in the bigger craft, who were in the air for twelve to forty-eight hours, got hot stew.

The last of the Lenabo soos was *NS11*, which flew 228 hours during the war and was kept on after the Armistice. It won its place in aeronautical history by chalking up a world-record endurance flight. The date was February 1919. Four months later it was lost at sea with all hands.

Lenabo is twenty miles from Aberdeen, just two miles south of the village of Longside, where the Rev. John Skinner, the poet of 'Tullochgorm' fame, lies buried in the same kirk yard as Jamie Fleeman, the laird of Udny's Fool. I have sometimes wondered what Mr Skinner would have said if he had seen the poetry that appeared in *The Battle Bag,* a magazine produced on the station.

For instance:

> If only all the kissing
> That takes place in Peterhead
> Were converted into football at Lenabo instead,
> There's lots of us would sleep a lot
> More soundly in our bed.

Then there was the one about the sport of parachuting on the station, 'Percy in a nice new suit, Took a trip per parachute – It wasn't me, and that's a mercy, R.I.P. to poor old Percy.'

When the war was over, the Lenabo base disappeared almost as quickly as it had sprung up. Some twenty years ago I took a trip to the old airship station to find out if anything was left of it. There wasn't much. I remember Charlie Heron of Longside, a partner in the firm taking timber out of Lenabo, taking me on a tour of the station. We wondered about the huge slabs of concrete, thirty feet by five feet, dumped in the grass and heather. Charlie thought they were the remains of windbreaks. We came on the remains of chimney stacks used in the making of hydrogen for the airships. When Charlie and his partner, Robert McGillivray, started work in 1966, both stacks were still standing – sixty-six feet high and ten feet wide. Not long after that, the army was called in to demolish the chimney stacks and the pillars at the gateway. The demolition of the airship station was carried out with such speed that it almost seemed as if Buchan wanted to wipe out the memory of how, when this peaceful corner became the front-line of the U-boat war, a whole community vanished.

My old friend the late John Reid, better known to the public as David Toulmin, wrote about this in his book *A Chiel Among Them*. The families there, he said, were 'uprooted leaf and branch'. John lived in a chaumer on the farm of Auchtydore as a youth.

At that time [he wrote], Lenabo was an exposed wilderness of uprooted concrete and a shamble of red bricks, like a devastated city, and from the hangar floors you could scoop up handfuls of lead and zinc washers that had fallen from the corrugated iron roofs during demolition. One ghostly farm had survived the holocaust, still intact among its native trees, at the foot of Torhendry, and even in those days the ivy from the broken windows was meeting in the middle of the stone floor in the kitchen, while the rusting gantry still hung over the peat fire, and there were broken milk basins on the flagged shelves of the dairy, a sad reminder of departure, a contented family uprooted by the senseless necessities of war.

Happily, Toulmin's book provided a record of the 'lost' Lenabo families during the First World War. He wrote about the Emporium, run by James Rae, the local shoemaker, who had a croft on the fringe of the estate. The general merchant's business was run by Mrs Rae and later by her daughter Edith. He reeled off the names of farming

The Lenabo memorial. Many local people, like Mr and Mrs G. Williams, from Longhaven, walk on the air station paths.

families – Hastie, Kidd, McShea, Smith (the tinsmith) Sangster, Nicholl, Davidson, Duffus, Logan, Reid, Penny and Robb.

> Through the nineteenth century [he wrote], they had lived in splendid isolation on the bleak expanse of Lenabo, their meagre requirements supplied by the 'shoppie' at the crossroads, growing their own crops and digging peat as fuel from the desolate bogs of Torhendry, until their lonely habitat was chosen as an airship lair.

He gave glimpses, too, of their lives: of Mr Lawrie of Easterton having his boots soed [sewn] and one heeled, which cost him thrupence ha'penny, while his daughter had her boots heeled and tongued, which 'stung the poor dear half-a-crown'.

I went back again to Lenabo recently. The old airship station was a wilderness, with tracks winding through it that are now used by walkers. But near the entrance, half-hidden in the bushes, was a memorial marking the site of the station. It had been erected by Longside Community Council in 2003 and it told how there had been 1,500 personnel on the base, supported by an infrastructure of shops, swimming pool, theatre, church and its own gas works.

'Visible for miles,' it said, 'the large buildings housing the airships extended to 150 metres long by 30 metres high. Concrete foundations, anchoring blocks and various ruins are still visible.' The plaque also carried a plan of the station, showing the hangars, repair and maintenance sheds, a hydrogen-producing plan, the billets and the station sick-bay.

I thought it a pity that there wasn't a picture or a replica of an airship on it, reminding visitors of the days when the Lenabo soos went lumbering over the green fields of Buchan.

21

KINGDOM OF FORGUE

The Forman Hill rises on the Aberdeenshire–Banffshire border above the River Deveron. It is the highest hill in the Kingdom of Forgue, and it was crossed by Mary Queen of Scots in 1562 when she went north by a hill road that is still known as the Queen's Road. I went up that ancient track on a cold, windy day that still had the bite of winter in it.

I was thinking of the name of this shapely peak, or rather of its two names, for it was known as both Forman and Fourmen. The name Fourmen Hill still appears on some up-to-date maps, and over the years people have argued over its real name. If you go back to 1794 the *Statistical Account* will tell you that its Gaelic name is *For-mon*.

Then there is the intriguing theory that it was named Four Men because the lands of four lairds met at the top of the hill. Charles Horne, who in 1903 wrote *The Kingdom of Forgue* under the pseudonym of Herd Loon, had a more imaginative version of this. 'The four lairds,' he wrote, 'agreed to erect a table on this spot, right up on the top of the hill, and have one jolly good dinner, each laird sitting on his own ground eating off one table – hence the name of the hill, Fourmen Hill; now called Forman Hill.'

Ordnance Survey maps show the site of a laird's cairn on the Queen's Road, so the Herd Loon's story may not be as fanciful as one would think, but there are no details of that meeting on top of the hill. Did servants really carry a table and chairs up to the top of that 1,128-ft hill so that their masters could have a jolly dinner?

Maybe, maybe not, but James Macdonald put a damper on such curious ideas in his *Place Names in Strathbogie*. 'I think the name comes from *fuar* [cold] and *monadh* [moorish hill],' he wrote. 'The name "Cold Hill" is most descriptive of the Forman, which during a great part of the year presents a bleak appearance from every point of view.'

He said that the name Fuar entered into many place-names, as in: Mead-fuar-vounie (Inverness-shire) the 'hill of the cold moor'; Fourknocks and Fourcoil (Ireland) the 'cold hill' and the 'cold wood'; and *feur-bheinn,* an ordinary Gaelic phrase meaning 'cold hill'.

The four lairds on Forgue's Cold Hill made up only a fraction of the lairdships in the Kingdom of Forgue. In the 1850s there were no fewer than twelve lairds there. They were an odd lot. The Corse laird was 'a rough, godless kind of man' who is said to have come across the Devil when he was out on Watchman Hill. He fled in fear and after that he always went to church on Sundays. The youngsters had a rhyme about him, 'Ali Pasha o' the Corse – The devil's ill, but he is worse.'

On the other side of Watchman Hill was the laird of Drumdollo. 'He was an eccentric sort of a creature,' wrote Herd Loon. 'He would have ordered two of his men to hold up his breeks while he stood upright in his bed and jumped into them. If his legs went right in, he rose for the day, but if his legs did not go right in he took to his bed again.' Then there was a bachelor laird at Bognie, a little below Bognie Inn. He was a stout, jolly, old man who had a pretty, stout hussy of a housekeeper who thought nothing of taking a muckle stick over his back if he displeased her.

The Frendraugh estate stirs memories of the ill-fated feud between the Crichtons and the Gordons, and a quarter of a mile to the east is the hamlet of Templeland, the home of the Shands. The laird of Templeland was 'a kindly old gentleman' who also had an estate near Inverurie. Farther south is Auchaber, whose laird, according to Herd Loon, was a good old-fashioned individual who was kind to his servants. When they went off in their carts with stacks of corn to Portsoy or Banff he would warn them, 'Dinna forget your big quites, although it is a fine nicht ye dinna ken fat it may be or ye come back.'

Up on Forman Hill, shivering in sympathy with James Macdonald's 'Cold Hill' theory, I was looking down on the River Deveron as it swept majestically through the Kingdom of Forgue. I have often wondered how this quiet corner of Aberdeenshire came to be called a Kingdom. Nobody seems to know. The author Nigel Tranter thought that it came about because of the powerful Frendraught influence. Herd Loon decided it got the title because of its size, agricultural richness and scenic beauty.

As far as I know, the only name that has ever been heard in connection with the Kingdom is that of Alexander Shand, of Templeland, who was a well-known agricultural improver and became known as the King of Forgue. I can't help thinking that he might have been one of the four lairds enjoying a jolly good dinner up on Forman Hill. But I tend to leave the last word to the place-name expert William M. Alexander, who, mentioning that 'The Kingdom of Forgue' was a phrase occasionally to be heard, added 'No one has any explanation to give of it.'

I have my own thoughts on who deserved to be called the King of Forgue – the laird of Cobairdy. His name was James Allardyce and he was the man who put Forgue on the map – and sent a whiff of *uisge beatha* floating away to Auld Reekie. He was not strictly speaking the laird of the estate, but he had a life lease of it. Everybody called him Cobbie.

The mansion house of Cobairdy sits in the shadow of Forman Hill. Its original name was Culbardie, *cul* meaning a hill back, and it was there that Cobbie formed a company with the aim of building a distillery in Glen Dronach. Two hundred years ago a colony of rooks nested in the woodlands at the Dronac Burn, their raucous cries warning illicit distillers that the Excise men were about. The rooks were still caw-cawing when the Glendronach Distillery was opened in 1826, but by then whisky-making had become legal.

The whisky was brewed and stored in the bonds until Cobbie thought it time to get some of it sold. He sent a traveller out on the road, but he made little headway. He was sent out again in another district, but he came back empty-handed. 'Well,' said Cobbie, 'There's no use us brewing whisky if it can't be sold. I'll go out myself and sell it.'

Cobbie made for Aberdeen, taking a barrel of whisky on his gig. He walked the streets of the city with a bottle of whisky in one hand and a dram glass in the other, begging people to taste his 'guid Glendronach whisky'. The canny Aberdonians drank the free nips, but they were slow to order it, so Cobbie went south to Edinburgh with his barrel, bottle and glass. He had some success in the Canongate. He took people back to his hotel room to taste his whisky, among them some dubious ladies who were out to sell their own attractions.

On the day before he left for home, he gave a flagon of whisky to the women. Herd Loon told what happened after that. 'In about an hour or so a certain street in Edinburgh was seething with drunken women going about holding a dram glass in their hands, crying "Tak' it out, it's good Glendronach whisky," and when anyone went into a public-house they asked for Glendronach whisky.' Cobbie sold all his stock before he left Edinburgh, and for many a year after placards were to be seen in nearly every public-house bearing the inscription 'Guid

Glendronach Whisky'.

Whisky, *uisge beatha* [the water of life], was never very far from people's minds – or mouths – in Herd Loon's time. He told what happened when the farm at Newmill of Pitfancie, one of seven meal mills in the parish, changed tenants. The machinery of the mill, which belonged to the outgoing tenant, had to be removed. The new tenant said to his herd loon, 'Laddie, they'll be needing us to give them a lift with the wheel. Tell them it can't be moved without a bottle of whisky.'

The old tenant did ask for a lift with the wheel and when they went to move it a 'little impudent nickum', standing with his hands in his breek pouches, cried out 'That wheel won't come out of that without a bottle of whisky.' The old tenant produced the bottle and the wheel was lifted. The 'impudent nickum' was Charlie Horne, the Herd Loon, and the new tenant was his father.

Whisky was also an essential commodity at funerals. Charlie Horne told of an old woman, Jeanie Rennie, who lived in a house built of divots [sods] or feal [turf]. When she died a barn was cleared out and a long table erected and covered with white sheets. Bottles of whisky, dram glasses and biscuits were then laid from end to end on it. Charlie, who was then a child, watched everything that went on.

> It was not one glass that was drink, but a good few [he wrote]. A man here and there around the table stood up and said something, then they all drunk and hurrahed. One man – James Adam was his name – stood up and spoke a good while, then he said 'Let us drink,' and with a loud cry he exclaimed 'Three times three – hip, hip, hurrah!' the whole of the company standing up and joining in the hurrah.
>
> I was somewhat startled with this kind of ceremony and drew back from the barn door, watching them come out at the low door like a swarm of bees from a skep, and they lifted the coffin with the remains of poor old Jeannie and carried it to the churchyard of Drumblade, and laid her in her last resting place.

Charlie, the Herd Loon, was born in the shadow of Watchman Hill. Here a watch was kept to spy out the Highland hordes when they came down to plunder the lowlanders. From the top of the hill you could see steamboats sailing up and down the Moray Firth. His book carried a section of poems. In them he wrote about how, after long years of absence, he came back to the cottage that snuggled 'close by the hill called the Watchmount [sic]'.

He stood looking at the walls, 'grim with age', and at their tiny windows, he saw the old barn and byre and the kailyard, but it was the door of that old cottar house that held him. As he stood gazing at it a feeling passed over him that he had never felt before. He thought he could hear the voice of his mother crying 'Charlie, come here!' But then, he said, he awoke from his mid-day dream.

In his book, he recalled how he had revisited the scenes of his youth – and about his disillusionment.

> The last time I was in Forgue [he wrote], the people seemed to be half asleep. There did not seem to be half the merriment and life that was obtained in my young days – only, the most of the folks were strangers to me and I to them. I could not help thinking had there been a few men with energy like that of old Cobbie, the shriek of an engine and the thunder of a railway train would have been heard in the Kingdom of Forgue long ago.

As I wandered about Herd Loon's old haunts I wondered what he would have thought of the changes that had taken place in the Kingdom in the century since he wrote his book.

22

ROYAL SALMON DINNERS

Aberdeen is a city where people lived life to the full in the good old days. That was two centuries ago, when the town was awash with societies and clubs bent on holding extravagant social functions, wining and dining until they were gorged with food, drink and gossip. It was called the age of conviviality.

George Walker, a local bookseller and author of *Aberdeen Awa'*, said that all ranks and classes 'formed themselves into congenial coteries, meeting in inns at all seasons and hours'. They gathered at county club soirées, at regimental balls and synod and presbytery dinners. At elections, 'immense assemblies were treated to good cheer, and would not disperse until they were thoroughly soaked'.

Then there were the masonic dinners (there were nine Mason Lodges in the city) and there was a celebrated wine club run by 'an antiquated Guildry', while the Incorporated Trades offered 'sevenfold hospitality'. The opulent Friendly Societies were to the forefront, including one set up by the booksellers. Walker himself joined it in 1838. 'The age of conviviality in Aberdeen,' he said, 'had not quite died.'

The Friendly Societies had fanciful names like the Narrow Wynd (the name of a street), the Wigmakers, the Dyers, the Independent Friends and the Blue Gardeners. The Blue Gardeners had an annual procession through the town, pausing at the Aulton where they 'drank a glass', and then returned 'to dine and spend the evening with decent mirth and hilarity'.

For those with gourmet tastes there was only one place to go – the Lemon Tree tavern, which was run for fifty years by Mrs Jane Ronald, who was famous for her suppers. Magistrates and clergy used it as their houff, which gave it a very respectable air. In 1813, a pamphlet entitled 'The Synod', published in Edinburgh, told how, when the synod met at Aberdeen many of the clergy went to dinner at Mrs Ronald's, 'digesting their wrongs'. It went on 'And now methinks at four I see the brethren all in "Lemon Tree" – for here, they fail not to convene, round Ronald's smoking hot tureen.'

William Carnie, journalist and musician, wrote about the Lemon

Tree in his *Reporting Reminiscences*. 'For half a century there had been no better known, no more comfortable hostelry in our city,' he said. 'It was frequented by the best of the town and county, and the hostess, old couthie, courteous Mrs Ronald, was held in the highest, the friendliest esteem by all her patrons.' He had a special word for Mrs Ronald's cooking. 'There never was seen, one might swear, such creamy Finnan haddocks, such magnificent partan claws, as Mrs Ronald was wont to place on the table,' he said.

Curiously, there was no mention in *Aberdeen Awa'* of another hostelry, the Royal, where for more than thirty years an event was held that stood high in the city's social calendar. There were no Finnan haddocks or partans served up at this function, for this was the annual Royal Salmon Dinner, held at the start of the salmon season. Carnie said he had seen on special occasions over two hundred gentlemen seated around the Royal Hotel tables, among them the leading citizens from lord provosts down. 'You may be sure they had the best of the prized February fish,' he added.

The Royal was the principal hotel in the city in the early half of the nineteenth century. In 1811, Archibald Simpson designed Numbers 40–44 on the north side of Union. In 1812, there were new buildings on the south side near Putachieside. Numbers 57–65 were to become the Royal Hotel and it was to this site that Lord Cockburn, the circuit judge, paid a visit in 1853. His lordship, who had a fiery tongue (he once said that the Duke of Gordon's visage on his statue in Aberdeen looked as if it had been rubbed over with oatmeal) was not well pleased. 'We had a beastly circuit on a sanded floor,' he said, 'and came away eagerly this morning from the stinking Royal Hotel.'

Beastly it may have been to Lord Cockburn, to others it was anything but that. It was known far and wide as Machray's, and the man who gave it that name was Isaac Machray, a sharp, hard-headed businessman who, as well as drawing an élite company to the Royal, was chief proprietor of a mail and stagecoach service which ran alongside the hotel operation in Union Street.

Carnie wrote about how this part of Union Street was 'astir with the departure of the mail coaches, the Union, the Defiance, the Duke of Richmond, with their snorting four-in-hand greys under the skilled care of the Cooks (Charlie, John and Alick), Davy Troup, one of the earliest coachmen, Tom Gray, John Rattray, Howatt (the bugler), cheerily starting north and south with their full complement of passengers.'

The names of famous coaches appeared in announcements of their departure times from the Royal. 'Defiance leaves the Coach Office, 65 Union Street, every lawful morning at 6 a.m., and arrives in Edinburgh via Forfar, Perth and Queensferry, at 8 p.m.'

Isaac Machray died in 1856 at the age of fifty-six. He had served as a member of the town council for a short time and was greatly interested in agriculture. He had a sharp temper, but a kind heart. He often gave a free 'lift' on an outside coach seat to working-class folk who had sick or dying relatives living at a distance from Aberdeen.

His successor was David Robertson, a model and popular landlord according to Carnie. It was said that there was 'no better purveyor of a first-class dinner than Robertson. Through him, the brawest of Highland lord, lairds and ladies made the hotel their passing home.'

But there were problems – one of the big Royal functions backfired on Robertson. New colours had been presented to the Royal Aberdeenshire Militia by Lady Saltoun and in celebration of the event the regiment gave a grand assembly in the Royal Hotel. More than 200 guests were there, including the élite of the city and county families.

Lord Provost Blaikie, the town clerk John Angus and other leading officials were there, enjoying the supper and dancing, and nobody noticed the time. The result was that the evening stretched beyond the limit laid down in what was called the Forbes McKenzie Act. There was a great fuss about breaking the limit and David Robertson was charged in the police court with keeping his hotel open to a late hour. A trial was held, with a police superintendent called Watson reluctantly appearing as prosecutor, and the *Herald* published a hard-hitting article about the whole affair.

'There is not in the city a more zealous and upright servant than Mr Watson,' it said, 'yet through this abominable Act, and some of its sour-faced abettors among the police commissioners, he was placed in a most humiliating position.' There was a weak bench of magistrates sitting in judgement. One of them, a mild, kindly, old gentleman, was said to be specially weak in his grammar, although it is hard to see how this affected the case. James Duguid Milne and James Collie, the two advocates defending Robertson, made a great deal of fun out of the case in their examination of the witnesses. They were probably still laughing when the verdict was given, for Robertson wasn't carried off to a dark cell – he was given a fine of twenty-five shillings.

There was no such trouble in 1860 when the Royal Salmon Dinner came round again. It had more than usual *éclat*, said Carnie. Lord Provost Alexander Anderson was in the chair, with the editor of the *Herald* as his croupier, and among the speakers were Sir Andrew Leith Hay, Sir Thomas Blaikie, Colonel Leith Hay and Baillie Morrison, Edinburgh. 'Mine host Robertson outshone himself,' said Carnie. The menu was 'twenty dishes of boiled salmon, ten dishes salmon cutlets, six dishes *vol au vent* of sweetbread, ten roasts of beef, four saddles of mutton, two rumps stewed beef, six turkeys, six beef-steak pies, ten lobster salads, twenty dishes of game, twenty dishes of mince pies, and so on *ad lib.*'

'But while the greater convivialists thus feasted,' Carnie noted, 'smaller fry did not forget themselves.' The coachmen of the city and neighbourhood held their annual supper – and the entertainment was said to be excellent. 'The nicht drove on wi sangs and clatter,' Carnie wrote in appropriate equestrian style, 'and it was not till a pretty late stage that time tightened the reigns of enjoyment and put a curb upon the hilarity and harmony of the proceedings.'

The Royal's famous salmon dinners kept it in the forefront of the social scene for many years. Even the birds knew about the dinners. When a big function was due to take place, live turtles (turtle doves) could be seen stalking about in the entrance.

The hotel's popularity began to decline when a rival opened a hotel at the foot of Market Street. Its host was Thomas Douglas, who had been the favourite head waiter at the Royal. Tall and strongly built, wearing Highland dress, he had more of a regal bearing than that of a master of ceremonies. Douglas prospered, but the tide of fortune ran out for David Robertson.

Changes came to the Royal buildings. A post office was opened at the south-east corner of the hotel, but it eventually gave way to a market that was being built – the Royal Galleries department store. 'The galleries, it will be seen, are on the principle of an arcade,' said a report on the project, 'and will form a tempting promenade for those of our citizens making purchases of "the good things of this life", for which our city has been so long famed.'

The Galleries store was taken over by Falconers and finally by the House of Fraser, who extended it but retained the arcaded look on the ground floor. No one now remembers the salmon dinners. William Carnie's plaintive cry comes echoing down the years. 'Where be now your famous dinners?' he asked. He said that Isaac Machray and David Robertson had been 'courtly caterers for the citizens, rulers and ruled, in the times that are no more'.

23

THE LUMS

A stone chimney stack can be seen sticking up in a field on the road from Tomintoul to Grantown-on-Spey. It seems to be the remains of a house, but a closer look shows that the lum is all that is left of the building. A few miles farther on is another solitary chimney stack – a duplicate of the first lum, with no sign of a wall or any foundation.

For years I passed these curious 'lums' on my way to Speyside. They were called the Fodderletter lums, taking their names from two farms on the Tomintoul–Grantown-on-Spey road. I often wondered what the original buildings looked like and why the ruins amounted to no more than a shattered fireplace. I was offered some unlikely theories, including one that the empty fireplaces were used by deer-hunters to gralloch [disembowel] deer they had shot. Then I discovered that the answer lay on the road I was driving on.

The Foderletter 'Lum', a shelter built by roadmen
constructing new roads in the Highlands.

In the early days of road building the roadmen had crude huts for shelter. Robert Southey, in his *Journal of a Tour of Scotland 1819*, told how he found road workers at Garve in Ross-shire housed in tents with 'huts of branches for their kitchen'. They were said to be 'miserable huts'. In the 1920s and '30s little had changed, except for one thing – the Fodderletter lums. The men had portable wooden huts which they set against the chimneys, the fires were lit, a meal was cooked, and then they stoked up the logs and settled down for a night's sleep, Next day they would be out on the road – knapping. This didn't mean that they were having forty winks; the word 'knapping' meant stone-breaking for the roads they were building or mending. This was done with long-handled hammers called stane-knappers.

Southey told how the men working under the engineer Thomas Telford carried out this job.

> The plan on which Telford proceeds in road-mending [he wrote] is this: first, but this is not essential, to level and drain; then, like the Romans, to lay a solid pavement of large stones, the round or broad downwards as close as they can be set; the points are then broken off, and a layer of stones broken about the size of walnuts, laid over them, so that the whole are bound together; over all a little gravel if it be at hand but this is not essential.

It seemed that the roadmen of the early twentieth century were following the methods of the Romans who had pushed their way north to Scotland. But I didn't have to go back to the Romans to find out about stone-breaking. When I was in Knockando I was shown a memorandum by John G. Shand (see chapter 11), a local man who wrote about the people in his parish, among them a roadman called Roddy Jock, who worked there breaking up stones for road repair.

> His stock-in-trade [said Shand] consisted of one short, heavy hammer for cleaving the heavy stones; one slender, long-handled hammer for reducing the broken stones to the desired size, one pair of wire gauge goggles and a large shovel. We marvelled at Jock's dexterity but learned that the knack was to find the line of cleavage – whatever that may be – and the hammer would do the

rest, provided of course you had the patience of Job and the arms of Samson and emitted the roadman's grunt as you applied the hammer to the stone.

Murray Cameron, historian at the Tomintoul Museum for seven years, told me that examples of the stone knappers' work could still be seen near the second Fodderletter lum on the Grantown road. This lum is taller than its partner and someone has painted a Scottish Saltire on one side of it. On the other side of the road I could see two or three heaps of small stones left by the stone-breakers. From where I stood they seemed a little larger than walnuts.

Murray took me behind the museum to see another leftover from the road-building days. It was a huge scraper with two heavy tines for cutting into the road. The scraper, the Fodderletter lums and the knappers' stones were all reminders of Telford's great battle to bring an efficient transport system to the Highlands.

The packhorse bridges, an earlier means of communication in the Highlands, have mostly all vanished, but some remain to show us how our forebears travelled about the countryside. There is, for instance, still a double-lumped bridge at Glenlivet, built about 1700, and now providing a lovely setting for a picnic site, as does the one at

Murray Cameron, Tomintoul historian, with a huge 'Scraper' used for cutting into the old roads.

Aberlour, which was repaired at a cost of five pounds in 1729. The strangest packhorse bridge I have ever seen is a double-storey bridge in the Braes of Enzie. The original lower storey of the bridge was used by packhorses.

The packhorse bridge had no place in Telford's plan – those days were gone. Telford was concerned about the lack of bridges over the main rivers. General George Wade had made thirty to forty bridges in the Highlands, but they were comparatively small. The commissioners for Highland roads and bridges were tight-fisted with their expenditure. 'Farthing wisdom', Southey called it.

Local landowners had proposed a site at Craigellachie for a bridge to span the Spey, and Telford approved. There was an appeal for subscriptions. It said that it afforded 'a favourable and noble opportunity of snatching from a watery and untimely grave hundreds of their fellow creatures, for the number of lives which are annually sacrificed in the passage of this rapid and impetuous river excel all belief'.

So Telford's Iron Bridge was built in 1815 at a cost of £8,000. Its single cast-iron arch crosses the 'impetuous' Spey and connects Banff and Moray in one great leap from the right bank to the base of the rugged Rock of Craigellachie. Two round battlemented towers rise up on either side, 'anchoring' Telford's triumph – this 'fairy-like struc-

Packhorse bridges in the Highlands have mostly all vanished. The bridge above – a double-lumped bridge – was built in Glenlivet about 1700.

ture', as Dr Cuthbert Graham described it.

There was a short right turn at the rock face on the Moray side of the bridge and motorists had to be careful, but it is no longer a problem. Times change, and cars no longer pass over the Craigellachie bridge. In 1972 it was bypassed and a new road was built a little to the north. It lies like a wounded giant, its double towers glowering defiantly at the folk who come to see it.

It has carried thousands of people over the Spey, it has opened new routes for a growing army of visitors, and it has withstood every gale and storm that Mother Nature has thrown at it – even the Muckle Spate. In 1829, when other bridges were being destroyed or washed away, the worst that happened to the Craigellachie bridge was that the iron arch with which Telford had spanned the river hung almost by a thread.

In 1994 a parade was held on the bridge to commemorate the amalgamation of the Queen's Own Highlanders and the First Gordons and a plaque was put on the bridge to mark the event. It was probably the last official ceremony to take place there. Now the oldest surviving iron bridge in Scotland has become a tourist attraction, looking down on one of the loveliest corners of the country.

Telford's Iron Bridge with two round battlemented towers rising up on either side.

24

A RECTORIAL RIOT

'Street Turned Into Battlefield' … 'Ugly Episode in Aberdeen' … 'Police Use Batons in Clash with Students'. The headlines were splashed across the front pages of Aberdeen's newspapers. The word 'riot' spread through the town like wildfire. They said nothing like it had happened since the 'bobbies' had used their 'sticks' during Communist–Fascist clashes in 1938.

The scene of this 'ugly episode' was the Upperkirkgate Bar, a favourite drinking howff of university students. The year was 1952. It should have been a great day for Aberdeen University – a new rector was to be installed, and then, in true traditional fashion, he was to be carried to a public house in the Upperkirkgate to share a pint with the students. Instead, a row broke out that set the whole town talking, rumbling on long after the installation was over.

Half a century has passed since that hit the city. I was a newspaper reporter at that time and got caught up in the mêlée. Recently, I was reminded of it in an old book about Aberdeen events in the nineteenth century. One of the chapters carried the heading 'University Rectorial Installation Riot'. The date was 1861.

So there had been two Installations hitting the headlines, separated by half a century. I wondered how they compared. I was in the City Bar when the story broke, a pub where John Baird was mine host and a homely waitress called Babs served up pints to thirsty journalists, academics, and CID men from Lodge Walk.

The new rector was Admiral Sir Rhoderick M'Grigor, the First Sea Lord. His installation went well. 'I had been given a grand hearing by the students during my address,' he said later, 'and we had been having lots of fun.' What followed wasn't fun. The trouble arose when the students attempted to follow the traditional custom of carrying their new rector shoulder-high to the nearest public house to toast his health.

There were students inside the pub drinking their pints and waiting to greet the rector, while others stood outside the robing room at Marischal College chanting 'We want M'Grigor!' When he appeared, the crowd gave a great cheer and broke into the strains of 'For he's a Jolly Good Fellow'. The next move was to the pub, but the police stopped the procession and a police sergeant and constable escorted the rector to the students' union.

Meanwhile, other police officers had barred the entrance to the pub and the angry students rushed forward in an attempt to force their way in. There was a fierce, confused struggle in which snowballs were thrown and police caps were knocked off. The reply to this student aggression was unexpected – the 'bobbies' drew their batons! Between twenty and thirty policemen were involved in the struggle with the students.

'The Upperkirkgate was turned into a battlefield as students locked with the police in Aberdeen's worst episode for many years,' reported the *Press and Journal*.

Inside the pub it was almost impossible to move and an attempt was made to clear the entrance for the students outside. Sir Rhoderick eventually returned to the scene from the students' union and was admitted to the public house. A cheer went up as he took his place behind the bar. The police then allowed a number of people to leave the bar, but outside hundreds of students were shouting protests and throwing snowballs at the police.

When the rector left the pub to go to an official lunch the trouble flared up again, sparked off by the arrest of a student wearing a University Air Squadron uniform. Four policemen surrounded him and his fellow students closed in on them in an attempt to free him. The police were given the order 'Sticks out!' Shouts of 'Fascists!' were heard and a shower of snowballs found their target.

Outside Lodge Walk, policemen formed a human barricade as the horde of yelling students crowded around them. Two more students in a dispute with constables were marched inside the police office. 'Free our men!' shouted the students. Principal R.V. Jones went inside the police office to discuss things with a chief superintendent and when he came out the crowd had dwindled. The remaining protesters disappeared when Professor Jones spoke the magic words, 'Come and have a drink with me.' R.V. Jones always had a 'mouthie' – a mouth organ – in his pocket, which he produced on appropriate occasions. Whether or not he soothed the students' savage breasts with a tune inside the Upperkirkgate Bar was never recorded, but he clearly played an important role in ending the Great Rectorial Riot.

The matter, however, didn't end there, for over 200 students at the university signed petitions to the Secretary of State for Scotland and the city's two MPs asking that a full public inquiry be held into the conduct of Aberdeen City Police after the installation of Admiral M'Grigor. The petitions claimed that 'batons were used against students without sufficient reason or warning' and that 'suitable action be taken against the officers found responsible'.

Later, the lord advocate, W.R. Milligan, announced that no action was to be taken against the five students taken into custody. It was the end of a strange affair that, as the *Press and Journal* said in a comment piece, evoked a sense of unreality. 'Such things,' it said, 'do happen, we all know but not in Aberdeen.'

Well, it had happened in Aberdeen before – nearly a century and a half ago. On 16 March 1861 the first rectorial election since the fusion of the Colleges took place. The candidates were Edward Francis Maitland, solicitor-general for Scotland, and Sir Andrew Leith Hay of Leith-hall. Sir Andrew polled 240 votes to his opponent's 202, but the system allowed the vice-chancellor, President Campbell, to have the final decision and he gave his casting vote to Maitland. This was regarded as an 'intrusion' by the students.

The installation of the rector took place on 20 March and this is what the *Aberdeen Journal* had to say,

> The agitation which has been kept up with more or less intensity among the students ever since the election seemed to be brought to a climax, in the case of those who opposed Mr Maitland, by the ceremony of his induction; for on entering the hall, greatly more than the wonted noise and excitement prevailed ... Not only did the usual variety of sounds – some of them comical enough – greet the ear, but also sticks were pitched about freely, without any regard to where they fell. No kind of missile, so far as could be seen, was allowed to be taken into the hall; but some of the malcontents had brought hammers or some kind of tool in their pockets, and they speedily smashed up the seats, and converted them into fragments quite handy for throwing about. The forms had been, as usual, nailed to the floor, but this did not prevent the operation referred to.

The magistrates and town council members, the professors and members of the university council, entered the hall with the lord rector to a cacophony of cheers, hissing, hooting and yelling, and a shower of sticks which fell 'without respect of persons or places'. Principal Campbell took his place at the rostrum and called on the meeting to engage with him in prayer. The response was more hooting and whistling, but when some calm was restored the principal commenced a Latin prayer. This was interrupted by 'ejaculatory sounds' which caused laughter.

The oath was administered to Mr Maitland, after which a protest against his election was read by a divinity student. The rector took his place at a desk to give his address, but when he beckoned for silence there was a hurricane of noise and he got no further than the first word, 'Gentlemen'. One student jumped on to a form and told him that the students didn't want him to address them.

The professors got down from the platform to remonstrate with students, but the hooting and whistling got worse, backed by some-one beating a drum. Handfuls of peas came hurtling through the air, followed by sticks and pieces of wood. The rector kept smiling and attempted to give his speech, 'Gentlemen, I accept – (cheers, hisses and interruptions) – as frankly as – (hooting) – the protest – (great uproar) – which you – (looking at the demonstrators) – have just offered' (uproar). The protest was handed to Principal Campbell, who received it and the rector tried again – 'Gentlemen, I should be entire-ly ——' (hooting and interruptions).

People near the rector noticed that blood was trickling down his face. He had obviously been struck by some of the flying missiles. The younger and quieter students tried to shame down the rioters and a voice was heard from the platform, 'Call in the police!' Principal Campbell moved to the end of the platform and warned the students that he would 'take other means to put an end to this disgraceful scene. The names of two or three gentlemen who have been taking an active part in these proceedings have been recorded.' There were cries of 'Out with them! Expel them!' The principal went on 'Your prospects in life are ruined by the proceedings today. Some of you not only make use of expressions of opinion but also use dangerous missiles.'

His warning had some effect, for some of the protesting students made a rush to leave the hall. The principal ordered the door to be locked, which was done. The police were sent for and several came up to the hall, but no force was used by them.

While students inside were now trying to get outside, other students outside were trying to get inside. Stones were thrown at the hall windows. The door was ultimately forced open and a number of students pushed into the hall. 'Pandemonium again reigned supreme,' it was reported, 'and the proceedings had perforce to be brought to an abrupt termination. The manuscript of the rector's address was handed to the press and a full report of it subsequently appeared.'

So ended the Great Rectorial Installation Riot of 1861. Whether or not some young students' prospects in life were ruined by the affair nobody can tell. For all we know, they may have gone on to become respected pillars of society – and their descendants may have joined the ranks of protesters in the rectorial riot of 1952.

25

DRUMIN MUSEUM

A massive ruined fortress, Drumin Castle, stands in Charlie Reid's tidy garden at Drumin Farm in Glenlivet. It was built in the fifteenth century by Alexander Stewart, better known as the notorious Wolf of Badenoch, and it was one of three strategically important castles built by the Wolf – the others being at Loch an

The ruined Drumin Castle, built by the Wolf of Badenoch, towers up in Charlie Reid's back garden.

Eilean on Speyside and Lochindorb on the moors above Grantown.

Charlie and Cathy Reid have become used to having an old castle as a garden ornament. They have never been over-awed by living in the shadow of this ancient stronghold for they themselves live in an imposing building which goes back to the early nineteenth century and holds its own niche in the history of the north. The farmhouse at Drumin was built in 1818–19 by William Mitchell, factor to the Duke of Gordon. James Skinner and subsequently his son, William Marshall Skinner, succeeded Mitchell as factor. James Skinner was factor to successive dukes of Gordon from 1824 to 1873 and his son from 1873 to 1904.

From the farmhouse you look across a courtyard to a long building whose distinctive entrance suggests that it may have been used as accommodation in the Duke of Gordon's time, or, at any rate, part of it. Today it is a museum of Scottish country life, run by Cathy Reid and her husband, an Aladdin's cave of curiosities, stocked with everyday items and unusual ones, from all over the north-east of Scotland.

Cathy was an only child, born on the farm of Templand near Rhynie. Charlie said that if you stood on the Tap o' Noth you looked down on it. Being an only child, she had to make her own entertainment, and she began to collect things that interested her. Like Topsy, it just grew and grew. 'What other folk threw away,' she told me, 'I

The farm buildings at Drumin have been converted to a museum packed with antiques and 'collectables'.

collected.' She could never have imagined then that her collection would one day range from royal dolls to toy soldiers, from a church organ to a horse-drawn hay turner from the 1920s, from poems and paintings to Victorian dresses.

There are some priceless items in the building, but it is really a museum of collectables, holding up a mirror to a way of life that has long since gone. It was Charlie who showed me round the museum. Cathy was ill at the time, but I saw her later. When I walked into the museum I felt as if I should stand up and sing 'God Save the Queen' for I was looking at a big picture of the Queen and Duke of Edinburgh, surrounded by royal dolls. 'She's a great royalist', said Charlie, 'not an anti-royalist.' There were royal albums and pictures all through the museum.

I moved off down a corridor whose walls were plastered with prize tickets from the Dufftown Flower Show and a poster announcing that the Fiddich and Dullanside Annual Gathering, 'under distinguished

The Royal dolls on display at the Drumin Country Museum.

personage', would be held in the field adjoining the Mains of Balvenie, kindly granted by Major Grant (was he the distinguished personage?) and entry would be by a gate near Dufftown railway station. There would be putting stones, a long race (one mile), a short race, a hop, skip and leap, an egg-and-spoon race and a grand tug-of-war. The date – 17 August 1898.

Up on another wall a small, round tin caught my eye. 'Fiery Jack', it said. Many years ago, when I was suffering from arthritis, someone told me to try Fiery Jack. I plastered it on hopefully and within a few minutes I knew why it had been given that name. My leg was on fire, burning so fiercely that I forgot the arthritis. I learned later that Fiery Jack was a counter-irritant. When applied to the skin it caused redness and heat, which distracted the brain from the original pain.

There were other medical items in the museum. Medicine bottles of all kinds were among the collectables, and here and there were poems and homilies about people's health. One of them was 'I really like my bifocals, My dentures suit me fine, My hearing is perfect, But Lord how I miss my mind.' Another verse seemed to be raising a banner against the Devil Drink, 'Since I'm sworn to live my life, To keep an easy heart, Some men may sit and drink apart, I bear a banner in the strife.'

If anyone was suffering from fear and disturbed sleep through too much liquor, there was a sure-fire cure for it – Baldwin Nervous Pills. There was a poster on these miracle pills, telling you how they would cure nervousness, irritability, stress, fear and dread, neuralgia, hysteria, disturbed sleep, melancholy, insomnia, and all nerve pain and diseases. The price was one shilling and a penny – two shillings and ninepence for a box.

When I was making my way through the museum I felt like someone being watched by ghosts from the past. Faces stared out at me from almost every room: a nameless soldier from some long-forgotten war, dolls sprawled round a cot, a big framed portrait of a lady who, I could have sworn, disapproved of my unseemly curiosity. There was even a picture of a dog sitting on a cart eyeing me up.

The whole thing had a distinctly Victorian feeling about it, emphasised by a dress worn by an attractive lady – a 'dummy' dressed in a long black gown, with an expensive necklace and a hat that would have put Ascot to shame. Cathy Reid told me that the 'dummy' arrived at Drumlin on the back of a coal lorry. There were other lovely dresses, among them replicas of royal wedding dresses.

The army was on parade when I was there – rows and rows of lead toy soldiers on a shelved frame, with others standing about lower down. Not far from them was a huge array of cigarette cards. Tin soldiers and fag cards were all the rage at one time. You either bought the cigarette cards or scrounged them off a passer-by, 'Any cigarette cards, mister?' Now they would fetch a good price in the collectable market.

The funniest item in the museum was a printed sheet that told the story of 'A Mistaken Impression'. This is the opening part of it. 'A young couple about to be married were both looking at a house in the country. After satisfying themselves that it was satisfactory they made their way home. During the journey the young lady was very thoughtful and asked "Did you notice any WC, Edward?" He hadn't noticed one so he wrote to the owner of the house asking where it was located. The ignorant, old landlord did not understand the meaning of 'WC' and came to the conclusion it meant Wesleyan Church and answered as follows:

Dear Sir, I have pleasure in informing you that the WC is situated about nine miles from the house and is capable of holding 230 persons. This is an unfortunate situation for you if you are in habit of going regular but no doubt you'll be glad to know that a great number of people take lunch and make a day of it while others who cannot spare the time go by car and arrive just in time,

There were other exhibits touching on such embarrassing matters: a row of chamber pots, or 'chunties', as we once called them, although *Chambers Scots Dictionary* prefers the more delicate 'chanty'. Maybe that's what they called them in the West End. One of the chamber pots had an intriguing inscription written around it, but I couldn't get near enough to read it.

Then there was the Flap. Hanging on a door was a long, droopy garment described as 'A lady's back flap combinations 1920 to 1930'. *Chambers Scots Dictionary* shied away from discussing combinations and flaps, but *Collins English Dictionary* said the former was 'a one-piece woollen undergarment with long sleeves and legs. Often shortened to combs.' We called them 'combies'. The dictionary didn't mention the flap, but it didn't take a great deal of imagination to figure out what it was for.

The final room in the museum stirred memories of my boyhood when I was taken to my grandfather's croft in Buchan. Here was the same fireplace, big and black, with a swey hanging over the fire and huge black pots waiting to be filled. There was a wally dog on the mantelpiece and a milk churn at the side, and hanging on the wall were a flauchter spade for cutting peat and a ditching spade. Nearby was an old school desk with a slate lying on it – and a slate pencil.

So that was Drumin's great museum of country life. If Cathy had been well, she might have come to the museum to play me out on her organ. This was an old organ she saw advertised in a magazine – an antique not a collectable. It was a lovely instrument, in good condition, and still playable. She got it for sixty-five pounds – a figure that my layman's mind thought was worth double or treble the price. It lay

This 'lady' with a fancy hat was a 'dummy' dressed in a black gown.
It arrived at Drumin on the back of a coal lorry.

outside the museum for a time because there was no room for it but it finally got a home inside.

They are friendly folk, these Reids of Drumin. They have been there for twenty-two years. Charlie, who is sixty-eight, likes folk. He delivers coal as well as running the farm and says he enjoys coal heaving more than anything else because he meets so many people on his round. They used to call him the Midnight Coalman because he often arrived home at midnight after his coal deliveries. He just couldn't stop chatting to his customers.

There was one more 'exhibit' to see before I took my leave of Cathy's museum – the castle. Charlie led the way through the garden, opening a gate that separated it from the castle. It had begun to rain and we took shelter under a huge arch, a vault. The Crown Estate was undertaking preservation work to stabilise the castle and improve access for visitors.

To the south-east, beside Glenlivet Distillery, there is another ruined castle on the edge of someone's garden. 'It's my extension,' joked Rosalind Stevenson, who lives at Schiehallion, in the shadow of Blairfindy Castle. The castle was built by the Earl of Huntly in 1586, probably as a hunting lodge. There are no visitors to this castle for it is in a dangerous condition. It is fenced in and behind the fence the

A fireside section of the display in the farm buildings at Drumin.

undergrowth has been allowed to go wild.

I left Glenlivet, sniffing the air for a whiff of *uisge beatha*, passing an old packhorse bridge that once had three arches but now only two. One was ripped away in the Muckle Spate of 1829. It has a lovely setting and there is a picnic site and a car park at the bridge. I was reluctant to leave this fascinating and beautiful area – and my friends, Charlie and Cathy, at their Aladdin's Cave.

26

THE GREAT CREMATION

Aberdeen turned its back on tramcar transport some fifty years ago. Buses were in, 'trammies' were out, their end marked by a spectacular parade through the city on 3 May 1958. Their 'cremation' followed a week later. Between 60,000 and 70,000 people flocked to see the last run. They lined the route from the Bridge of Dee to the King Street depot, cheering and laughing. There was little doubt that the old trams had a firm place in the affections of the townsfolk.

The cavalcade consisted of four modern double-bogey trams and two of the older type, led by William Hay, a sixty-year-old veteran driver of horse-drawn trams. They stopped at the Town House so that the official guests could alight, among them Lord Provost George Stephen, the provost-poet who wrote such couthy verses as 'The Nichts are Comin' Doon'. His journey in the cavalcade made it clear that the nichts were comin' doon for the city's tramcars. Among the other guests were Hector Hughes, MP, and members of the council and corporation officials, with wives and friends. They went into the

Bain's bus taken by George Washington Wilson.

Town and County Hall to wine and dine, while lesser mortals went on to the final stop at the King Street depot.

So that was the end of a transport era that went back to the 1870s, when horse-drawn buses clattered through the city, and pushed out to suburban areas like Bieldside and Bucksburn. They were Bain's Buses, run by an entrepreneur, William Bain, who was to dominate the transport scene in Aberdeen in the late nineteenth century.

Bain's Buses operated from the Old Waterhouse in Union Place, which was swallowed up by Union Street. The Waterhouse took in water from the River Dee at a rate of a thousand gallons a minute, then stored it and distributed it to Aberdeen's 75,000 population. When it became obsolete in 1866 it was occupied by Bain, who built stables and coachhouses behind it. It was there until after the First World War.

I have a picture of a Bain's bus, taken by Aberdeen's pioneer photographer George Washington Wilson. It is an elegant vehicle, double-decked, with a ladder at the rear to take people to the upper deck. A bowler-hatted conductor stands at the bottom of the stairs, with a ticket machine round his neck, and up on the open top the driver sits holding the reins, which run down to two well-groomed horses. On the side of the vehicle are the names 'Castle St, Rosemount, Mile End' and below them are other names obscured by the large wheels on the vehicle, with small wheels at the front.

Rosemount and Mile End are names that I knew well when I travelled on the Rosemount circular route as a boy. It was sometimes known as the Queen's Cross circular, which was understandable, for it was the hub of the tramway system in those early days. The Queen's Cross depot included a body repair shop, a foodstuff facility and a blacksmith's shop. It was on the west side of Fountainhall Road and eventually became Grampian TV's studios. Across the street, where the Denburn comes splashing down through open countryside, were the stables.

Lachlan Mackinnon, in his *Recollections of an Old Lawyer*, drew a vivid picture of Aberdeen in the days of horse-drawn trams. He told of how winter conditions played havoc with the new forms of transport. Snowfalls had not been heavy in the 1830s, but from 1870 onwards they were sufficient in frequency, quantity and duration to impede street traffic, and sometimes to paralyse it.

In December 1878 there were nineteen days in which no tramcar or omnibus could be run on snow or ice, and the same sort of record was repeated with variations winter after winter for twenty years afterwards.

> A heavy snowstorm [said Lawyer Mackinnon] being an occurrence that no human foresight could prevent, was left as an Act of God for nature to remedy and the snow was allowed to lie and accumulate until it should please the clerk of the weather to prescribe a thaw for the removal of it.
>
> Private sleighs were brought out and glided along the streets with jingling bells, bakers' vans might be mounted on runners, and wheeled goods traffic required the aid of trace horses even on the level. When tramcars or buses could not be run, the tramway company brought out rough wooden sledges, dragged by four horses on which some twenty of the public sat back to back and enjoyed for their money an element of sport and adventure in respect that, if the horses started the heavy sledge with a jerk, the sitters cannoned against each other from front to back, and half a dozen of them at the rear would be shot off into the snow.

Tramways were operating in many large towns, including Edinburgh and Glasgow in 1870. The Aberdeen District Tramways Company was formed in 1872. Lachlan Mackinnon's father was the original secretary and his son succeeded him in 1893. The tramways were opened to the public in August 1873, the occasion being marked by a procession through the streets of eight cars and twenty-four horses. A dinner was held afterwards 'with sanguine speeches'.

The total capital subscribed was only £18,240, and with this modest equipment of money and plant the company entered upon its enterprise of 'providing tramway locomotion for a population of 88,000 persons'. In 1874, about 1,200,000 passengers were carried.

Passengers driving to work in the new cars would have seen a well-known businessman passing them in a 'carriage and fine horses'. Inside it was Alexander Ogston, better known as Soapy Ogston, travelling from his home at Norwood on the outskirts of the city to his soap manufacturing factory in Loch Street. Whatever Soapy thought of the honking, rattling vehicles that shared the road with him, he took exception to one thing they had put in his way – snow!

In those days there was no snow-clearing by the town council, and the tramcar company decided to keep the cars running with their own snowploughs and by spreading salt on the track. It was not an ideal solution, for snow and cold slush were piled up in the sides of the streets. But, said Lachlan Mackinnon, it was a choice of evils – snowploughs and salt, or no tramcars.

The tram lines had by that time extended over many miles of the city and the public had come to depend on them for getting about in wet or stormy weather. Soapy Ogston, travelling to work in his fine carriage, was obviously not impressed by the argument. He raised an action in the Court of Session to stop the Tramways Company from transferring snow from the tramlines to the sides of streets and from putting salt on the streets. He claimed that the accumulation of snow by snowploughs impeded the wheeled traffic and that the salt freezing mixture injured the carriages belonging to himself and other users of the streets.

The judgement was made in favour of the company, but was reversed by the House of Lords in favour of Mr Ogston. The decision, said Lawyer Mackinnon, was 'right in point of law, but it was a hard blow to the company, as it cost them £4,000 of expenses, left matters just as they were, and pointed to no remedy'. In fact, it had the effect of stirring up the town council to do their duty in the matter of snow removal.

The tramway company also clashed with William Bain's company in 1888. There had always been a certain tension between the two competing firms, and it reached a climax when the tramway company took steps to have the single track in Union Street turned into a double track. Bain objected to it, arguing that there was too much traffic at Holburn Junction and the entrance to his premises would be obstructed. He had a photograph taken showing the junction so crowded with wheeled vehicles that it looked like Piccadilly Circus. Lachlan Mackinnon got the same photographer to take pictures of Bain's men washing their unharnessed cabs at this 'congested' street corner and Bain lost the case. The line doubling went ahead.

Bain's company was sold to the corporation in 1898, two years after the Tramway Company had sold their whole concern to the town. The corporation celebrated their 1896 take-over by decorating the trams with flags and by introducing a universal penny fare. With typical Aberdonian thrift they restricted the penny fare to two days. The total stock in the take-over was 3,399 cars, 244 horses, 2 blacksmith's shops and several horse buses.

By 1903 there were more than twelve miles of track, and in that year halfpenny fares were introduced in Union Street to encourage short distance use of trams. By 1911 the cheap fare covered all routes. The years rolled on and the trams and buses with them. In the final year of the trams the number of passengers totalled 11 million while the buses chalked up a total of 85 million.

In 1945 the Aberdeen city council met to decide which form of transport would be used in the future – tramcars or buses. The shortage of buses at that time determined the choice and the council decided that trams would continue to lead the way. Only one man voted against tramcars. He was T. Scott Sutherland, a fiery, red-headed architect who had only one leg and dashed around with a crutch like some latter-day Long John Silver. Between 1945 and 1950 the number of buses rose from 77 to 149, an upward trend that continued until the 1950s. But the writing was on the wall for the old 'trammies'. In October 1954 the No.5 trams were withdrawn from the Rosemount circular route, and in January of the following year the council decided that the whole of the tramway system should be abandoned by October 1959.

Aberdeen wasn't the first city to sound the death knell of the tramcar. In 2004, when moves were made to bring back the tramcars to Auld Reekie, Albert Morrison, a well-known *Scotsman* columnist, wrote about how the last tram in Edinburgh 'ground its way to oblivion' in 1956. Recalling what seemed to him to be golden days, he said that trams rode through his dreams like 'stately galleons sailing sedately along Princes Street among barging buses and vulgar freight carriers'. They were unlike the 'multi-coloured, rickety-as-rickshaw Glasgow ones that screeched like tenement stair squabbles'.

He made no mention of Aberdeen's tramcars. He probably thought that in this north-east corner we were still riding about in poshed-up carties. At any rate, he was too preoccupied by the fact that a Paris-based company, Transdev, had landed a £750 million contract to run the city's tram system. 'I have nothing against France,' he wrote, 'although its people live in a state of controlled tipsiness from the age of five, induced by vin ordinaire, do not love animals unless cooked, and only stop waving their arms to go to sleep.' He suggested that they 'import Gallic drivers, possibly short, blue-vested, beret-wearing people who could operate onion-festooned trams and steer with characteristic élan while in special compartments traditional, French, three-piece accordion bands played music in three-quarter time ... It could turn our trams into transports of delight,' he declared. 'If I am dreaming, let me dream on.'

If Aberdeen's city fathers are thinking about bringing back the trams as an alternative to turning the whole city centre into a pedestrian way, they might get some inspiration from Albert Morris' 'dream'. When, like Albert Morris, I summon up remembrance of things past, I have my own dreams about the 'trammies'. I remember, as a youngster, clambering eagerly up the steps of open-air trams bound for the beach, where the North Sea winds reminded you that this was Aberdeen, not Majorca. I remember, too, that some trams were fitted with cow-catchers, and I kept looking out for them to see if they had picked up an Aberdeen Angus cow on their travels. Trams ran down by Kittybrewster, where cows with wanderlust periodically broke away from the Mart and went rampaging through the streets. I also remember the tramcars rattling down George Street and coming to a halt at the end of the line with nowhere to go and no turning point. It wasn't a problem. The driver simply walked to the other end of the tram, adjusted the overhead electric connection, turned the right wheels, pulled the right nobs and off we went – back the way we had come. You couldn't do that on a bus!

Aberdeen's tramcars made their last official run on Saturday 3 May 1958. It began at the Bridge of Dee. About six o'clock in the morning ten-year-old Marjorie Fowlie, a pupil at the High School for Girls, headed a long queue of people who all wanted to get on board the trams that were open to the public. Beside her was a ten-year-old lad called Wesley de Leurere who wanted to ride on one of the trams because he thought they were 'better than buses'.

A crowd of about 2,000 gathered at the Bridge of Dee. The horse-drawn tram joined the cortege at Holburn Junction and a police car and two police motor-cyclists cleared the way down Union Street. Two white horses, Bloom and Tib, were the stars of the show. When they reached the King Street depot they were unharnessed and led into a horsebox. The old tram was pushed inside by a modern car and the others followed. That was it; as the local paper said, 'Our glory day was over.'

But there was one more ceremony to be performed, without the crowds, a week later. While Aberdeen slept, twenty trams rumbled through the streets on their way to the Sea Beach, where they were lined up on the private tram track before being cut up for scrap. More trams were brought from the Queen's Cross depot to add to the gigantic funeral pyre.

Few people saw the Great Cremation. Some Constitution Street residents heard the trams go past and got out of their beds to see the fire. One woman attended the 'funeral' because she had missed the farewell journey down Union Street. When the blaze had burned itself out, a man from a Stratford scrap firm began cutting up the trams.

That was the end of Aberdeen's 'trammies'. From time to time there has been talk of bringing back tramcars, but, whatever happens in Auld Reekie, it is unlikely that we will ever see those 'stately galleons' sailing sedately down Union Street. But, as well as George Washington Wilson's photograph, I have another picture that will always bring them to mind. It shows two tramcars on Union Street going in opposite directions.

The time on the Town House clock is 3.20 pm, Queen Victoria still stands on her pedestal at the corner of St Nicholas Street (the Bon-Accord Centre had yet to be built), and one of the cars, No.5, is coming down from the Castlegate on its way to the Rosemount circular route. On the other side of the street, opposite the Gloucester Hotel, passengers are boarding a No.1 Bridge of Don tram. To me, the No.1 tramcar was always the stately galleon and 'transport of delight' that Albert Morris wrote about, for it was on a No.1 tram that I proposed to my wife when home on leave from the RAF in 1945. When I was wed and demobbed, I left the old Rosemount circular route and changed to No.1 Bridge of Don, which took me to my mother-in-law's house, but in time we moved to our own home and were back on the No.5.

27

THE PACKMAN POET

Johnny Milne was a little man. He rode through the countryside on a donkey, hunched on its bony back like some latter-day Don Quixote, a big pack hanging from his shoulder. He wore knee breeches and a Tam o' Shanter bonnet, and if the weather was bad he wrapped himself in a grey plaid and wore a cap with flaps that came down over his ears.

He had worked as a shoemaker, a soldier, a postman and a pedlar, but it was as a writer of ballads that he made his name, singing them and selling them at feeing markets all over the north-east of Scotland. His faithful donkey carried him from cottar house to laird's mansion, up by Nochty and across the Ladder hills, down by the Don and back to town to sell his wares at the Market Cross. Nobody ever saw his donkey when he was in Aberdeen, for he reverted to 'shanks' mare' then.

They said he was 'the last of the old race of characters'. He was no 'patterer'. He recited his ballads and poems before selling them, which meant that he sometimes had to work his way through forty-five stanzas, or more. He usually wound up his presentation by saying, 'Now my lads and bonnie lassies, they're selt for a penny the piece, or twa for three bawbees.'

Johnny was born at Dunnottar about 1792. His father, William Milne, who was a sailor, went off on a voyage to the West Indies and never returned. His mother died shortly afterwards. Johnny was sent to live with his grandfather, a blacksmith at Fetterresso, where he received his schooling. Later, he went to Aberdeen and worked as an ostler to an uncle who was a horseshoer in Bon-Accord Street, but left this to become a shoemaker. He then moved to Durris, where he lived by himself for three years until he married a woman from Glenlivet.

When Johnny had a spell of poor health after his marriage he decided to move to his wife's native place. Glenlivet was whisky country – smuggling country. It was almost as if the air reeked with the scent of *uisge beatha*. There were said to be 200 stills in the area at one time. It may seem an unbelievable figure, but when Alfred Barnard visited Glenlivet in the late nineteenth century he was told that 'formerly smuggling houses were scattered on every rill, all over the mountain glens, and at that time the smugglers used to lash the kegs of spirit on their backs and take them all the way to Aberdeen and Perth for disposal'.

Johnny Milne must have thought that soutering was a dull way of making a living when you could set up an illicit still and go into the whisky-making business. That's what he did, despite the fact that he preached temperance in some of his latter poems. It was in Glenlivet that Johnny found his aptitude for rhyme-writing, although he had tried his hand at it when he was eighteen years old. It may have been because he was caught up in the romance of whisky smuggling, but, that apart, he also used his verse to tilt at the hated excisemen. It was after he had a run-in with the excise authorities that he wrote his first lengthy piece, 'The Highland Lads, or Noughty Glens'. The poem ran to thirty-seven verses, which he said he composed between breakfast and dinnertime. It described battles between whisky smugglers and gaugers, and said that the excisemen were sent out by Lord Fife and other proprietors – 'our gentlemen surveyed the hills, and sore destroyed the smuggling stills'.

'Burn no more bothies in Mount Sack,' it warned. Mount Sack was Socach, which takes its name from the Gaelic *soc* (snouty hill). There are two hills in the Strathdon area, one near Glenbuchat and the other south of the Water of Nochty. Although the 'highland lads' detested the excise, they held no grudge against the King. The final verse read: ' May George IV the crown long wear, May all his enemies disappear, And his loyal subjects his heart cheer, Among Britain's Isles in the morning'.

Johnny gave up smuggling about 1828 and went on the road with his pack and his poems. He did this until well into his sixties, when the years began to catch up on him. He was known at farms and crofts far and wide and had a particular affinity with the farming community. If they had a grievance they only had to tell Johnny and he would take up their cause – in rhyme.

He was never afraid to challenge authority, as his Noughty poem showed, and he had a gift for sarcasm that hit hard at his opponents. A Radical in politics, he wrote a number of political squibs, which brought him into conflict with a Colonel Sykes, as well as Lord Fife and many other country gentlemen. He detested the great Sir Robert

Peel and made him his target in a number of rhymes, such as 'Sir Robert Peel, the turncoat chiel, Head of the Tory faction, Doth boast he'll mak' the kirk to feel His mighty poo'er in action'. For about forty years he wandered about fairs and markets all over the north-east, but in 1868 he retired to a son's house at Cullerlie, Echt. He must have had intimations of immortality when he wrote the following verse, 'There's nothing sure to you or me Beneath the moon, But only that we baith maun dee – Lord kens how soon'.

It came to him in January 1871. Today, he is forgotten, for he was not a brilliant versifier. There was a touch of the McGonagall about his poetry, and it was said that you had to hear him recite his rhymes with his own peculiar drawl to appreciate them. His best-known poem was 'The Deil o' Baldarroch, or the Banchory Ghaist'. Baldarroch is a farm on Lower Deeside, near Crathes. The poem began,

> Some time ago I heard a story telled
> Aboot some fouk that had amaist been felled
> At Baldarroch, wast frae Aiberdeen –
> The like for mony a year there hasnae been.
>
> The evil spirit – to his name rebuke –
> Took up the hauntskip in the fouk's peat-neuk;
> Afore the fire fouk couldna sit for fear,
> For peats and clods cam' bungin' ben the fleer.
>
> The bere-beater, of great wecht and size
> Aff like a bird into the air did rise;
> It flew ower the houses like a lark,
> And down on the fouk's taes fell wi' a yark.
>
> The fouk gave out that everything was lost,
> The verra cheese ran to the fire to roast,
> The fouk were terrified where nocht was seen,
> For ika thud was like to blin' their een.
>
> An' 'cause they daured him wi' the Word o' Gweed,
> He drave the very house maist heels owerhead,
> He split and bursted ilka pot an'pan,

The fouk, through fear, took to their legs and ran.

The steels an' chairs in heaps o' boords were ca'd
The very wheels got tee, and ran like mad;
Baith oot an' in the fouk were clean bombased,
An' far an' near the country was amazed.

The awful cloddin' scarcely e'er devalued,
Until at last the parson he was called;
The parson cam', an' gained the hoose wi' prayers,
But still the clods were thuddin' here and there;
An' when the sun went down they grew mair thick;
The fouk saw naething til they faun the lick.

The haunting of Baldarroch took place in 1838–39. News of the ghostly goings-on quickly spread – 'an' far an' near the country was amazed' – and people came from all round the area hoping to see Auld Nick at work. Rumours were rife. Missiles were said to rain down on unsuspecting heads, washing was pitched on to the roof of the house, and it was whispered that a milk churn had rolled out to meet the farmer and danced a jig around him.

The seventh baronet of Leys, Sir Thomas Burnett, ordered an investigation and the laird's brother and a kirk elder met witnesses in the farm kitchen. James Thomson, a mason, swore that the strange happenings were authentic. 'When I was sitting here last night,' he said, 'I saw the spurtle come through that stone' (here he pointed to the bimney brase) 'and fly butt (through) the house, and while I was taking snuff there came a stone through the ceiling above me and shut my snuff box and bruised my fingers to boot.'

'I was sitting upstairs in the garret last afternoon,' said William Downie, a ground officer on the estate, 'when I observed an old shoe running in the crap of the wall, but when I tried to lay hold of it I was unable to stop it'.

There were two different versions of how the Baldarroch story ended. One said that the finger of suspicion pointed to a servant girl, the other that the farmer went off to Buchan to seek the advise of 'Doctor' Adam Donald, the Prophet of Bethelnie (see chapter 9). The 'Doctor's' prescription was unlike anything that would be given today.

He told the farmer that when he got home he should get hold of a white cock, draw blood from it, then liberate it. This, he said, would banish the evil spirits from his premises. Whether or not the Prophet's white cock advice was taken up remains a mystery, but the spooky incidents were eventually traced to a servant girl. When the local minister spoke to her the 'hauntings' stopped.

Willian Skene published 'The De'il of Baldarroch' in his *East Neuk Chronicles*. He knew many of the pedlar poets who sold their wares at the Market Cross in Aberdeen's Castlegate, and it is certain that he knew Johnny Milne. He said that Johnny was 'one of the old minstrel worthies', that he was often to be seen 'with a delighted crowd of rustics around him' and that 'The De'il of Baldarroch' was his best-known poem.

The farmhouse of Baldarroch stands on a minor road branching off the main North Deeside road at Crathes. I went there to see the haunted house, half-expecting to see spurtles and shoes come hurtling over my head when the door opened. Carol and Stewart McGuire have lived at Baldarroch since 1991 and it seemed as if the De'il had left his mark on it. Carol had felt a sudden drop in temperature and a 'cold, creepy' atmosphere in the byre and some outbuildings, and her husband had felt the same. They didn't worry about it: they had stayed for seven years in a former mill in Lanarkshire where the ghost of an old man made regular appearances.

A similar story was told about a farm in the parish of Lonmay, named Boodie Brae, which was the cause of the proprietor leaving his farm. You can read about Boodie Brae in the next chapter.

28

BOODIE BRAE

The Buchan village of Longside nestles in the centre of a spider web of roads near the South Ugie Water. If any village deserved to be called a 'curiosity', it is Longside, if only because if was originally known as New Peter. Nobody seemed to know who Peter was, or even if there was a Peter.

But there were other curious things that drew me to this corner of Buchan. They say that many of the old streets and lanes have retained quaint names, but if you want to step into the past the best place to go to is the old kirk yard. There is a roofless church there, dating from 1620, which once claimed to have ten doors, but there is some doubt about it. It could have been true, for they had odd ways of preaching in those days. The Rev. John Skinner, of Tullochgorum fame, preached from the window of his cottage at Linchart, near Longside, when his Tiffery church was burned by Hanoverian troops in 1746.

Skinner, who died in 1807 aged eighty-six, is buried in the old kirk yard, and not far from him lies Jamie Fleeman, the laird o' Udny's fool, whose last words still come echoing down the years, 'Dinna bury me like a beast.' Jamie's shrewd replies to people who mocked him make you wonder if he was as half-witted as most people thought. 'Fa's feel are you?' he asked one tormentor. He was buried in an unmarked grave, but in 1861 an Aberdeen man who was visiting Longside to see John Skinner's burial place heard that there was no stone on Jamie Fleeman's grave. With some friends, he raised enough money – £14 – to erect a pillar of Aberdeen granite, with the inscription: 'Erected in 1861, to indicate the grave of Jamie Fleeman, in answer to his prayer "Dinna bury me like a beast." So Jamie was buried decently as he wished, but what happened in later years must have had him whirling in his grave. It was the most curious story of all the Longside tales.

Nothing, it seemed, could ever disturb the peace and tranquillity of little Longside, yet in 1822 an event occurred that stunned the whole community. It happened at a croft less than a mile from the village.

The croft was called Braehead, but after the curious happenings of 1822 it became known as Boodie Brae.

I first heard of Boodie Brae in a tract held by William Walker, author of *The Bards of Bon-Accord* and a collector of chapbooks. Walker had twenty tracts in his collection, covering a variety of subjects, but it was Boodie Brae that caught my attention, for I knew that the word 'boodie' meant a ghost, a hobgoblin and object of terror.

The story of Boodie Brae was told in a scarce booklet called *A Descriptive Account of the Formartine and Buchan Railway*. In the old days, locomotives from the Formartine and Buchan Railway came puffing up the line from Peterhead, heading for Mintlaw and the main line to Aberdeen, but the tracks have long since gone. The line is now a walkway. The writer of the booklet was David Grant, author of that rollicking poem 'The Muckle Spate of Twenty-nine'. In it he wrote about his journey through Glen Ugie and of coming to 'the meandering green-margined Ugie'.

> After looking backward to the right and seeing the bridge of Crooked Neuk, with its two substantial arches carrying the turnpike over the Ugie, if we look to the left we will see the once-famed and far-feared Boodie Brae. The two crofts we now pass and which, as will be noticed, are pleasantly situated on the brae opposite the forenoon sun, and sheltered from Borean gales by the Ardlawhill wood, were originally called Braehead, but now Boodie Brae, from a marvellous occurrence there, which at the time created a great sensation far and near.

The choice of the word 'marvellous' to describe the events at Braehead seems ill-considered, for it was a cloud of fear that hung over the folk of Longside. David Grant, instead of dismissing it as mere superstition, said that someone in league with Satan had 'raised a great disturbance at the croft by means of the Black Art'.

The tenant at Braehead, a James Wylie, was said to be a very respectable and decent individual who had been at the croft for a considerable length of time. But when Auld Nick knocked on his door, his life became a misery. 'From the disturbance, the frights and the nightly fatigue it entailed on Mr Wylie, during the six months of its duration, for it operated nightly for about that length of time, the poor man got the beginnings of his death,' wrote David Grant, who got his information from a neighbour at Braehead. 'The infernal agency employed was invisible, but the effects and operations were palpable.'

People from all corners of the north, some from great distances, came nightly to Longside to 'see its freaks'. To show Grant what an alarming affair it was, his informant related the events on one particular night, when he and four other men and an old woman went to watch the spooky proceedings.

We went in the gloaming to the house and seated ourselves. Mr Wylie went to his bed. Up till midnight nothing was seen or heard, but about the dead hour of night strange unearthly sounds were heard within and without. As it had been the custom of tormenting Wylie in his bed by tossing him up and down and denuding him of the blankets, the woman we brought with us, devoid of fear, went and seated herself at the bedside, remarking that she would fain see the power that would *tirr* [strip] the man in his bed when she held the blankets.

Diane Norrie at her house in Braehead, once known as Boodie Brae. Part of the old cottar house still remains.

She had scarcely taken hold of the bedclothes, however, when out came one of the pails of water and after cutting some capers emptied its contents around her, while at the same time all the blankets in the bed were lifted, as if by their own accord, and tumbled out of the bed upon the floor with great force, and everything in the house moved as if there had been an earthquake.

Chairs and tables danced through the house; the crockery danced in the plate rack on the wall, the potato-chopper, which hung on one end of the plate-rack, mounted as if by magic and came and struck me a severe blow on the cheek. At the same moment, two of the other men were levelled on the floor, one by a severe thud on the forehead by peat, and the other by a blow from a luggie-cog [a bowl with a handle] that came from the *rances* [wooden posts] of the kitchen-dresser.

The four men searched every corner of the house, expecting to find some mortal who was the cause of the uproar, but they drew a blank. 'Everything,' said Grant's eyewitness, 'was in motion and flying in all directions through the house, and the poor man was walloping up and down in his bed and screaming fearfully, and so was the woman we brought with us, her bravery having fled and fear overtaken her when she saw the pail of water move ben from the door and empty itself upon her.'

Some found the house 'too hot to live in' and ran out, but others remained. The commotion settled down for about an hour, but then started again and went on till morning. New parties went to watch every night, but nothing could be done to stop the 'clodding [pelting with missiles] at Wylies'.

'Even doctors and ministers came with bibles under their arm, but were exposed to its fury, as were other people. All were convinced that Beelzebub was at work in the house and the place. It was not till Wyllie left the place and died soon after that there was peace and quiet within the walls of the dwelling of Braehead, since that time known as Boodie Brae.'

There are no ghosts and ghoulies, no boodies, haunting the braes of Longside now. The name Boodie Brae stuck for a long time, and even appeared on maps, but when I was there a big sign on the approach to the house read 'Braehead.' Everything has changed. The house has been extended and altered, the grounds beautifully laid out, and a big conservatory built. Even Mr Wylie would have slept happily in such a home.

Diane Norrie, her husband and two youngsters came to Longside twelve years ago from Perth. Diane took me round the back of the house, where you could see part of the old cottar house, which hadn't been changed. What did she think of the 'great sensation' that had set all Longside talking – and shivering? Diane had never even heard of Boodie Brae. There are no pails of water flying about the house nowadays, no bedclothes tossing people up and down, no crockery dancing, no strange unearthly sounds.

I wonder what Jamie Fleeman would have said about it all. Nearly two centuries have passed since it happened, and there is no real explanation. It might have been a trick played on poor Mr Wylie, or it might have been a touch of mass hysteria, or, as David Grant said, it might have been Auld Nick himself, raising a disturbance at the croft by means of the Black Art.

I left Braehead and made my way down to the main road, down to the 'meandering green-margined Ugie', where I looked across to the brig of the Crooked Neuk. There used to be a local distillery there producing Glen Ugie whisky, but in the mid-nineteenth century it 'fell into decay'. Maybe that was the answer, maybe the good folk who

A board telling the story of Jamie Fleeman.

gathered to see the Boodie Brae's 'freaks' had sampled too much of Longside's *uisage beatha*. No one will ever know…

Jamie Fleeman, the Laird o' Udny's fool, was buried at Longside.
This is the memorial raised to him in the cemetery.

29

PACK BRIDGE PROVOST

The Old Pack Bridge stands a stone's throw from the River Dee on the south approach to Aberdeen. It was built in 1693–94 to take travellers over the Pot Burn, a turbulent stream tumbling down into the Dee and it replaced a wooden bridge built in 1541. There seems to have been a rough bridge even before that, for the six-inch Ordnance Survey map shows at the burn mouth a 'Plank Bridge 1523'.

The official entry in the burgh records on 7 March 1541 reads 'The haill Counsell ordains the maistris of the brig wark to byg [build] ane bryg of tre [wood] our the Potburne on this side of the brig of Dee and to get and by al thing necessar thairfore and ordains him to caus raise ane gravatour [officer] to course [search] for all stuff sic as lym, tymmer and jrm [iron] taken away fra the brig wark.'

The present brig linked the Hardgate to the Bridge of Dee and on to the historic Causey Mounth. Built with three arches, it became redundant when Holburn Street was laid out, but it was kept in repair as 'a memorial of antiquity'. In 1923 it was moved a short distance east of its original site and was rebuilt with stepped parapets, which completely changed its appearance and character. No heavily laden pack horses could cross it now.

So the old brig stands rather forlornly in a cluster of trees on a path leading to the Bridge of Dee. The Pot Burn is now known by the less romantic name of Ruthrieston Burn. In the two spaces between the arches, shields bearing coats of arms were carved on blocks of sandstone. Vandals saw these as tempting targets for their stone throwing, with the result that it became impossible to make out anything in the shields and the inscriptions on the stones.

One of these fading stones carried the coat of arms of Robert Cruickshank of Banchory, who was lord provost of the city in the late seventeenth century. Few people walking over the old Pack Bridge nowadays would know anything about him or about the curious tale that lay behind the stone.

Provost Cruickshank, who was born in 1623, married Sarah Leslie, daughter of an earlier lord provost, George Leslie. The couple had five sons and six daughters, and also in the household were 'two servant lasses, each of which gets sixteen marks of yeirly fie, and ane man servant who gets twenty-four lib per annum'.

George Leslie, who was provost from 1685 to 1687, made a considerable fortune in the business world (he left a thousand marks for 'decayed and indigent burgesses of Guild'), but he was almost robbed of his chance to sit in the provost's chair by a curious royal decree. It said that only the king had the power of naming the magistrates of all his burghs 'as oft as may be considered good for his service'.

Although this 'Divine Right' was nothing less than usurping the rights of burgesses, they had to accept it, but on the day Leslie would have been elected a letter from the lord chancellor arrived recommending him to be provost – 'as a command from the king'. This procedure continued through Leslie's term of office. Lord Provost Cruickshank would probably have faced such problems with a good deal more vigour. He was a strong-willed man, a 'masterful provost', which was a polite way of saying he was over-bearing and intractable. 'He took his own way,' they said. Cruickshank wore the lord provost's robe from 1693 to 1696 and there were rumblings in the council about 'the unfair means' taken by him to hold on to his office, getting himself elected several years on succession. More bad feeling was created by the methods he used to get complete restoration of the Presbyterian religion in the town.

The plaque on the wall of the Pack Bridge.

Not content with putting his own stamp on the city's affairs, Cruickshank took steps to see that his name would live on after he had gone. When the Pack Brig was moved and rebuilt, he arranged – without the sanction of the council – to have a stone with his coat of arms (three boars' heads) built into the brig. What made matters worse were that they were not his coat of arms. Dr John Milne, a local historian, had this to say about it in his book *Aberdeen* in 1911,

> He presumptuously caused a stone bearing a shield with three boars' heads cut off at the neck to be built into the east face of the bridge. These arms had been registered by some person of the name of Cruickshank and, though the provost had no more right to take his neighbour's coat of arms than his coat of cloth, he passed them off as his own.

The Provost's action stirred up an even greater hostility among the majority of council members. Their reply was recorded in the Register of the Council in 1698.

> The councill, finding that when the bridge of Ruthrieston was rebuilt by Robert Cruickshank of Banchorie, being then (1693–4) provost, he did clandistenly cause put up his armes in the said bridge without any act of concil, albeit he contrabute nothing for building thereof, and that the same was begune and near ended in Provost Cochran's time (1691–2) and was builded on the money of the Bridge of Dee, doe therefore apoint the said Robert Cruickshank's armes to be taken down and to be given to him, he paying the pryce thereof and appoints the Mr of Kirk Work to cause put up in the place where the said armes stood ane handsome cut stone with the following inscription, viz: *Senatus Abredonensis Hunc Pontem Impensis Ex Aere ad Pontem Dee Spectante. Extruendum Curavit, 1693.* [The town council of Aberdeen caused this bridge to be built with money from the Bridge of Dee Fund, 1693.]

The provost, not surprisingly, refused to pay anything for the stone and the council went ahead with its plan to replace it. There was, however, no Morayshire sandstone in Aberdeen and the inscription was carved on the inner end of the old stone which had Cruickshank's coat of arms on it. It was then turned outside in and put back on the bridge.

When Cruickshank finally retired and gave up the civic chair he fired a final parting shot at his critics – he put up his son-in-law, John Johnston, as his successor. At the election a large number of council members stayed away, which meant there was no quorum. Cruickshank overcame this problem by going out from the Town House and taking 'burghers off the street' to cast their votes. Johnston, out of a leet of three, was chosen provost.

A number of councillors, headed by two baillies, Thomas Mitchell and John Allardes, protested and applied to the privy council for redress. The allegations made against Cruickshank said that the endeavour to get his son-in-law elected was an attempt on Cruickshank's part to continue to hold the chief power in the council. It was also said that Johnston was a professed and open enemy to the established religion, that he did not believe in capital punishment, and moreover that he was a member of that 'detestable sect' called Quakers. It obviously worked, for a decree of the privy council dated 25 November set Johnston's election aside.

Provost Cruickshank is said to have 'long survived the affront'. Perhaps he had mellowed, or he may even have regretted some of his actions. At any rate, as the years slipped away so did the hostility against him. In 1705 the town council ordered the stone to be turned again to show the arms and gave instructions that an inscription be carved below them stating that Robert Cruickshank of Banchory was provost when the bridge was built.

The *Senatus Abredonensis* inscription can still be seen on a plaque on the north side of the bridge, but time has completely obliterated two inscriptions on the opposite side. Now, there is nothing there to show that Robert Cruickshank was provost of the city when the bridge was built, no mention of the three boars' heads, no indication that this 'masterful provost' had been rejected by his peers – and been taken back into the civic fold in his declining years.

30

MEGRAY FAIR

Upon a hill in Urie lands,
Near by Stanehive a Market stands,
It bears the name of Meagra Fair,
To which the Counties round repair.

The village of Cowie, once a royal burgh with a royal castle, has long since vanished from the Mearns landscape. It lay to the north of Stonehaven, and how it slipped into oblivion is something of a mystery. But the ruined kirk of Cowie still stands in its ancient graveyard below the local golf course.

It was to that old kirk yard that I went in search of the man who wrote the 'Meagra Fair' poem. His name was William Kilgour, and he lived on a small croft on the estate of Urie. He was said to be 'a natural genius'. He worked as a weaver at Glithnow for sixty-two years, turning out bedcovers and tablecloths. He was also a clockmaker – most of his clocks being made of wood.

Kilgour, who composed a number of poems, died in 1837 at the age of eighty-six in the same house in which he was born. He was buried in Cowie churchyard, where a tombstone was erected to his memory. The inscription on it read, 'By his friends: Here lyes the man, for aught we know, That liv'd and died without a foe, Now mould'ring here beneath that clod, An honest man's the noblest work of God.'

The hill of Megray was the scene of the 'Raid of Stanehyve' in 1639, when the royalist forces of Viscount Aboyne were defeated by the Covenanters. About ten miles to the south-west is another hill, Herscha Hill, where 3,000 head of cattle once gathered for the famous Paldy tryst. Here, vinters' tents stretched over the hill, fires blazing behind them and broth pots swinging on their tripods. Blind fiddlers and pipers scraped and skirled a tune, and legless beggars pleaded for a coin or a crust of bread.

Those were the days when more than half the parishes in Aberdeenshire had their fairs and markets. William Alexander, in his *Place-Names of Aberdeenshire,* listed fifteen fairs and two trysts in east

Aberdeenshire and seventeen fairs and fourteen markets in west Aberdeenshire. He added five markets on upper Deeside which had the Gaelic names recorded.

Truel, Andersmas, Cowin, Mary, Tanglan, Braycock, Anna ... these are only a few of the place names that hid a wealth of information about the great fairs and markets of the past. The Trewel or Truel fair, held at Kennethmont, took its name from St Rule, patron of the parish, while the Cowin fair preserved the name of St Congan, the patron of Turriff. The Andersmas fair was held at the Cross at Old Rayne, and the Tanglan fair was at Tanglandford, a well-known crossing of the Ythan at Tarves. 'Tanglan is a corruption of St Englat, the tutelar saint of Tarves,' wrote Dr John Pratt.

The crossing was an important point for cattle droves in the seventeenth and eighteenth centuries. Ten thousand head of cattle were said to have crossed the Tangleford in a single day. They were not going to the Tanglan fair, but to Aikey fair at Old Deer, which by the end of the eighteenth century was one of the largest in the north of Scotland. Generally, more than 500 horses came to Aikey Brae.

Tarland had seven annual fairs or markets: the Bryak fair at Martinmas, the Yule market in January, the Horse market in March, the Rood fair at Whitsunday, the Cow market in the week after, Luaf fair in July and Lammas market in August. These annual fairs often ended in cudgel fights. The Birse men would clash with the Strathdon men, or the Leochel–Cushnie men would do battle with the Aboyne men, and more often than not the Tarland men would take on all and sundry. They were called the Tarland Tykes.

> You'll find as good as e'er drew bluid,
>   To fight in Tarland town man;
> Knock down their foes wi' hearty blows,
>   An' nobly craw their crown, man.

> Our Deeside boys mak' little noise,
>   They ken our Tarland laws, man,
>   They needna come to try our han'
>   At clubs or shak' o' fa's, man.

The St Laurence fair, better known as the Lourin fair, which ranked alongside the most important horse and cattle markets in Scotland, took place at Old Rayne. It matched Tarland for its broken bones and bloody heads, for it was a boisterous, bawdy affair which saw 'many a bloody racket'. It had its place in north-east ballad lore in a song about a woman who lost two of her lovers there, 'The tane was killed at Lourin fair, An' the ither was drooned in Dee.'

Old Rayne was the home of Charles Leslie – 'Mussel-mou'd Charlie, – a chapman poet and ballad singer. He lived to the ripe old age of 105, dying in 1782 (see chapter 5).

St Sairs or St Serf's fair was held at Culsalmond, about four miles from Insch. In 1682 it was at Monkeigie, now Keithhall, where St Serff was the patron of the church, but it was later moved to Culsalmond. In 1924 there were about 500 horses at the fair. The register of the Great Seal records that in 1591 there was 'Sanct-Sairffs fair at Wranghame, a farm near Colpy'.

The name Wranghame is pronounced 'Rangem' or 'Vrang-em'. Although the Poll Book of Aberdeenshire in 1696 and other records at that time show the name as Wranghame, the Ordnance Survey map gives it as Wrangham and Old Wrangham. It is a curious name, but one explanation is that it is Old English for 'home'.

The fairs of that time had more to them than the mere selling of horse or cattle. They were enlivened with entertainment by singers such as Mussel-mou'd Charlie and wandering performers with merry-go-rounds and shooting galleries, and by sellers of home-made tin and wooden wares. There were tents and stalls for the sale of sweets and refreshments.

The Mary fair was comparatively small, but its organisers at least tried to introduce a novel note to the proceedings. It was held at Newton of Auchindoir twice a year, in spring and autumn, until about 1822, when it was moved to the village of Lumsden. The Newton farmer was obviously glad to see the last of it, for he offered a prize that would be awarded at its new site in Lumsden. This was 'in consequence of the annoyance to which he was subjected at the time of the market'. It had been the practice to give a prize to the best-looking servant girl who attended the feeing market. The gift was a flower – a lily with a pound note wrapped around its stalk, and the winner was dubbed the Flower of Mary fair.

The Sleepy Market at the Hill of Christ's Kirk near Insch was said to be one of the most notable markets in the seventeenth and eigth-teenth centuries (see chapter 34). Other big fish in the fairs' pool were Aikey Brae and Old Rayne, where clumping Clydesdales still maintain the tradition of the old horse fairs.

Alongside the giant fairs were the minnows, among them the Donnan fair at Auchterless, the Skeir Thursday fair at Old Aberdeen on the Thursday before Easter, the Ruid, Rood or Red fair at Ellon and the Mid Lentron fair at Banchory. New Deer held two horse fairs, one in June, the other in October; one of them was known as Skippy fair. Before the St Sairs and Lourin' fairs there was a horse sale on the Burgh Muir at Inverurie called Charles fair. About 200 horses turned up. There was also a Michael fair at Aboyne, but it deteriorated into little more than an auction sale mostly for sheep.

In 1925, the *Scottish Notes and Queries* published a list of fairs that had vanished 'within recent times': St Donan's (Auchterless), Scuttrie (Craigievar), Bartle fair (Kincardine O'Neil), Pollander or St Apollinaris (Inverurie), Mary fair (Lumsden), St Denick's (Methlick), St John's (Strathdon), St Luke's (Tarland), Greenburn (Newhills), and Little Byth, Echt, Glass and Peterhead.

The coming of the railway and changing social conditions sounded the death knell of the old fairs. By the early years of the twentieth century many of them had been swallowed up in the weekly mart or monthly market.

31

JOCK THE GIANT

When I pass the Milton of Crathes on my way up Deeside I always keep an eye open to see if Jock the Giant is still there. For five years Jock has towered over the art galleries and craft shops at Milton, near Banchory. His huge feet are clamped down on the ground and his arms reach up above him, holding what seems to be a ball in his hands.

Not many people looking at Jock would think that he was once an ash tree. He was sculpted into human shape by Keiji Nagahiro, an artist from America, who specialises in tree sculpture. Born in Los Angeles in 1947, he has been living and working in Scotland since 1975. He married an Aberdeen girl, Marian.

His skill as a tree sculptor has taken him all over Scotland on commissions for wall sculptures and freestanding sculptures for private

The feet of a giant!

houses in Aberdeenshire. He has had commissions from such contrasting bodies as the National Trust for Scotland, the High Hopes Charity in New York State and the Garioch Amateur Swimming Club, and he has made a series of giant spheres in mixed woods for Harthill Castle. The first time I saw Jock the Giant he seemed to me to be a football player, leaping up to grab a wayward ball, although the ball didn't seem to have quite the right shape. Keiji had other exhibits inside the Milton Art Gallery and among them was a smaller version of Jock the Giant. He was holding a decorated bowl, not a ball, and he had Pictish symbols – one was the familiar fish symbol – on his body, and tattoed circles on his legs. These were Pictish symbols seen in Aberdeenshire. 'They came from the ancestors of the people here,' said Keiji. 'That's what interested me.'

Seeing Jock for the first time with the 'ball' in his hands, I jokingly asked Keiji what team he played for. Back came the reply, 'The Pagans!' That response shed some light on our friendly giant, for Keiji obviously saw his creation as a mythical figure, and not just a wooden cut-out of a football player. He had his roots in the folklore of the area.

Keiji lives in the Old Manse of Bourtie. It was near here that Robert the Bruce rose from his sickbed and routed John Comyn, Earl of Buchan, at the Battle of Barra in 1307. Barra Hill, which rises to 634 ft, is crowned by a circular Pictish fort, three acres in extent. It is known as Comyn's Camp and is said to be where the Earl of Buchan passed the night before the battle.

Keiji says the view from his house is priceless. He looks out on a landscape where history has left its mark wherever you turn, in crumbling ruins, old castles and ancient stone circles. The remains of a stone circle are scattered on the hill near the Kirkton of Bourtie. The recumbent is seventeen feet long and has one of its flankers still in place, while two circle stones and a jumble of boulders lie around it. The historian and author Nigel Tranter, writing about the Kirkton, which he thought was 'not particularly beautiful either without or within', was intrigued by a Pictish symbol stone, with crescent, double-disc and mirror-and-comb symbols built into the wall of the old graveyard, high up under the eaves. He thought it 'an extraordinary place to find such a thing'.

In 1992 Keiji made a copper and bronze Model Stone Circle for the Friends of Grampian Stones, a body set up to conserve and protect the antiquities of the north-east. Curiously, a carved stone ball, c.3000BC was found on Glaschul Hill at Towie on Upper Donside. It is now in the Museum of Scotland. Nigel Tranter described it as 'one of those peculiar Pictish carved stone balls'. I wondered if this was what Jock the Giant was carrying.

Different aspects of Keiji's work were shown at the Milton Gallery, both outside and in. Many were abstract. Keiji looks on trees as abstract. 'Many people don't really realise that,' he said. Two of his abstract sculptures at the Milton exhibition created a great furore. These were sculptures of a man and a woman, standing on their heads, or, to be accurate, on their necks, for they had no heads. 'There are a lot of upside down things,' said Keiji. 'Life is upside down.'

They were called Mr and Mrs, although during the Gulf War, when Scud missiles were used, they were called Mr and Mrs Scud. They were made from sycamore wood and stood outside the Milton Art

Jock the Giant on the site of Milton of Crathes.

Gallery. No one could have mistaken their sex. Nothing was hidden.

I watched some visitors look away when they passed, while others turned back and did a double-take. There were complaints from some people and they were condemned as pornographic. The newspapers descended on them. But there was a happy ending. The 'Mr and Mrs' exhibit was bought by a couple from Perth and taken away to a new home.

In 1998 Jock the Giant went on a tour with Scottish Sculpture, whose workshop at Lumsden he uses. He was installed at the car park in Milton Gallery in 2000. Keiji is a former committee member of Aberdeen Artists Society and regularly contributes to the annual exhibition. In 1997 he made a Sphere of Infinity & Japanese-Scots Sphere for the exhibition. His parents were Japanese.

Keiji Nagahiro, the man who makes giants out of trees, is content with his lot. He lives, he says, where the gods lived. From the Old

These 'upside-down' sculptures at Milton of Crathes caused some controversy.

Manse he can see the Mither Tap, the home of Jock o' Bennachie, who, in a battle with Jock o' Noth, hurtled a great rock at him that left its mark on one side of the hill and his fingerprints on the other side.

Jock the Giant should feel at home in the north-east for at one time there were more giants in this part of the world than you could ever imagine. When I was walking the hills I often heard stories about them, or was shown shadowy places where they had lived – or died. Up in lonely Glen Fearder on Deeside, beyond the Queen Mother's cottage at Auchtavan, was the highest farm in the glen. It was called Auchnagymlinn, from the Gaelic *Ach nan Comh-iomlaidean* [field of inter-changing – in other words runrig lands]. It was said to be a place 'long extinct', and it was destroyed by sand and gravel in the floods of 1829, washed away in the Muckle Spate.

It was there, I was told, that a giant had lived, the last of his race, and if I wanted proof of this I had to look for a grave twenty feet long somewhere above Auchnagymlinn. I never found it, although the ruins of the farm buildings were still there. Later, I learned that, according to tradition, there were giants of a kind there, a family in the forks of the Fearder Burn who were all seven feet tall. They all died young.

32

A TERRIBLE FURY

Gales, gales, gales ... they say they are all because of global warming. Back in 1876 nobody had ever heard of global warming, yet in two months of that year the north-east of Scotland was blasted by gales that nearly blew everybody away. It was, they said, a year that was memorable in the annals of Aberdeen for its serious disasters.

The first gale began on unlucky 13 November and continued intermittently for more than a month. Blowing hard from the south-east, it turned the sea into 'a tempestuous condition'. There were no shipping casualties on the Aberdeenshire coast at that time (they were to come later), but two English barques were wrecked farther south, one near Bervie, with the loss of seven men, the other at Johnshaven, with the loss of nine of a crew.

Earlier that year, in April, the Dee ferry disaster had shocked Aberdeen. The ferry, plying across the Dee between the city and Torry, was swamped and thirty-two lives were lost. Now, seven months later, the ferry-boat faced another disaster when it was carried down the Dee by the storm. It was saved only through being run ashore on the south side of the harbour entrance.

Nowadays, we sit in front of our TV sets and watch whole villages being evacuated because of flooding, but such evacuations also happened in 1876. There was extensive flooding in the Sugarehouse Lane district and no fewer than twenty-seven families, comprising seventy adults and about three times as many children, had to leave their homes and find alternative shelter.

Daniel Mearns, who joined the council that year and later became Lord Provost, set up a scheme to raise funds for the relief of people who were badly hit by the gale. Coal was distributed to storm-struck victims and bags of sawdust were provided to dry the sodden house floors.

There was a lull in the storm, but then the gale broke out again. Heavy rainfall made the situation worse and there was more flooding in the lower parts of the city. Up on the Buchan coast a Cromarty schooner was driven ashore at St Combs and a Peterhead schooner was wrecked at Kinnaird Head. Everyone on board the Cromarty vessel was drowned, but the six men on the Peterhead boat got off in safety.

December came and there was no let-up. An abnormally high tide hit the south breakwater, which was covered by scaffolding for extensions, and a succession of immense waves dashed against the hard masonry and swept in a continuous roaring cataract along almost the entire length of the works. The doors of the lifeboat house were burst open by the force of the seas and the lifeboat had to be moved. The upper stones of Abercromby's jetty were torn up and hurled along the channel, while a number of the larger stones were forced out of the north pier itself.

Little Footdee was pounded by the storm. The tide was so high that the waves came dashing against the houses in Fishers' Square, flowing over the roofs in some cases. It was said that terror seized the inhabitants. The only safe place for them was the church in the square. The Fittie folk retreated into the kirk, taking with them what furniture they could, and any other effects they were able to carry.

The scene inside the church was described in one report as 'ludicrous in the extreme – the pews piled up with cradles, tables, chairs, bedding, crockery and other domestic utensils, and sixty-one homeless men, women and children in desolate misery, condoling with each other in that the church at least was safe from the destructive powers.'

Outside, the storm raged on. The beach bathing station, which had been practically rebuilt three years before, was completely wrecked. The doors of the lifeboat house adjoining it were again forced open and the lifeboat was drawn out by the ebbing of the surf and knocked to pieces. The harbour dock-gates were also burst open by the force of the waves and made unmanageable. The abnormal amount of water which got into the harbour caused great alarm. The receding tide made many of the ships almost topple over, and others hung on their mooring chains in 'the most fantastic and dangerous positions'. Half a dozen fishing boats, insecurely moored, were carried down the channel and swamped or dashed to pieces.

Shipping along the Aberdeenshire coast was ravaged by the storm. The Norwegian-built schooners *Repart* and *Frederickshall* were both lost at Rattray Head and their entire crews perished. A Montrose steamer was stranded at Arbroath and a Swedish brig shared the same fate at St Andrews.

It seemed as if the storm would never end. On 20 December the wind came whistling off the sea again, gathering strength until a full-scale hurricane was battering the coast. Nothing like it had been seen in the north-east. The floods came back, bringing more damage to the harbour and to town property. Then came the snow, and the telegraph service was brought to a standstill.

A Norwegian barque was driven ashore at Belhelvie and the master and three of the crew were lost. One Norwegian brig tried to enter Aberdeen harbour, but failed to get in and was driven northward, finally striking the beach at the mouth of the Don. The seven men on board the ship got off safely, but when another Norwegian brig was driven ashore near the Donmouth the crew of nine were drowned.

The Grim Reaper was taking a heavy toll on this stretch of the coast. A foreign barque foundered off the Black Dog and all hands were lost, and when another brig struck the Belhelvie Sands the crew of eight were drowned, four of them while attempting to get ashore.

The crews of two other vessels which struck near Donmouth were able to get off safely except one man, who fell into the sea and drowned. Two vessels foundered near St Combs – there was no trace of their crews. Another two vessels struck the rocks near Cove, both foundering at the same time and carrying their crews with them. The same fate overtook a schooner at Newtonhill, when a crew of eight were lost.

There were several wrecks near Stonehaven and Wick, one at Lossiemouth, and seven on the Orkney coast. Mother Nature had come rampaging along the east coast of Scotland in a terrible fury, bringing down 'one long series of frightful disasters' on shore and at sea. In all, sixty-three vessels were known to have been lost, and the number of lives lost in those two months came to an appalling total of 294.

33

CONFESSIONS OF A COCKATOO

Cocky was a good soldier. He obeyed orders, got on well with his mates, regarded himself as a Highlander by adoption, and never flinched or faltered in the face of the enemy. 'I was something of a philosopher,' he once said. 'I accepted the inevitable.'

Cocky, of course, was no ordinary soldier – he was a cockatoo. I first heard of him some years ago when I visited Leith Hall, the National Trust for Scotland property near Kennethmont. There was a summer exhibition there called 'For King and Country, the military lairds of Leith Hall,' and one of the exhibits was a small book with the title *Confessions of a Cockatoo.*

The explanation given was that the cockatoo had been brought home to Leith Hall by Col. Alexander Sebastian Leith-Hay and had written its memoirs. Between the covers of this slim eight-page book was the incredible story of a bird that spoke both English and Hindustani, went into 'action' in the Indian Mutiny, and eventually settled down to a peaceful life in Aberdeenshire.

Leith Hall.

The initials 'CLH' on the book cover gave the game away. It was written by Charles Leith-Hay, who was a brother of Alexander Leith-Hay of Rannes, one of the fighting lairds of Leith Hall. Alexander served in Canada, fought in the Crimean War (he was in the famous Thin Red Line at Balaklava), and quelled the Indian Mutiny with his regiment, the Ninety-third Highlanders.

Through Cocky and his ghost-writer fascinating glimpses are given not only of the fighting in India but also of the colonel's attitude to what Cocky called 'one of the darkest deeds of history – the massacre of Cawnpore'. Cocky is clearly the colonel's mouthpiece.

> Never was a war more justifiable [he declares], never was a cause more congenial to the soldier than the Indian Mutiny. It was no acquisition of territory to gratify kingly ambition, no wholesale slaughter because monarchs had a difference of opinion. It was consecrated revenge for the foul murder of innocent women and children, and to crush the Hydra head of rebellion.

Cocky's background is a bit vague. He claims to have been born in the Australian bush, captured by a black man and taken by steamer to India. 'Many people came to look at me and all said the same thing, "Pretty Cocky!" which after a time I learned and articulated.'

He was sold as 'the pet of royalties' and was 'caressed and petted by beauty robed in silks, dazzling with jewels'. He was with the rebels at Cawnpore, where his part 'consisted of screaming (and cockatoos can scream) at the pitch of my voice'.

It was here that Cocky was captured by a soldier of the Ninety-third Highlanders and taken to Col. Leith-Hay. From then on he 'shared the hardships and saw the glories of that splendid regiment, the Ninety-third'. He was given a cage and a native bearer to look after him. He enjoyed 'the manly, honest laughter of the soldiers around the camp fires', but he spent much of his time in his master's tent. They became great friends.

At Leith Hall in later years he would remember all the battles he had taken part in and, he said, 'my old blood tingled in my veins'.

> On one occasion [he recalled] when the regiment was under very heavy fire, advancing to the attack, a round shot took my bear-

er's head off. As I was in my cage, suspended from a bamboo on his shoulder, the effect was somewhat startling, but beyond being a little shaken and swearing a good deal in both English and Hindustani I was none the worse.

The last action Cocky saw was the Battle of Burnilly, where Col. Leith-Hay was in command of the Highland Brigade. That victory brought an end to the Indian Mutiny.

Cocky went home with his master to the family seat in Aberdeenshire, 'The peaceful scene, the heather hills, the old trees on whose bracken I have often had an irresistible desire to perch, at first appeared a strange contrast to campaigning in India.'

He said that being with the Ninety-third Highlanders and spending the rest of his life in sight of the heather might not be a sufficient reason for calling himself a Highlander, but it made him one in thought and feeling. 'Why should not a cockatoo have thought and feeling?' he asked.

Alexander Leith-Hay retired in 1860 and succeeded his father in 1862. He married and settled happily at Leith Hall, with his feathered friend at his side. He died in 1900 at the age of eighty-two.

Confessions of a Cockatoo was written in 1896. There is nothing in it to indicate how much Charles Leith-Hay depended on his brother's recollections of the Indian Mutiny for Cocky's story. His main idea was that some people might be interested 'to hear from a warrior cockatoo his career (however imperfectly) written by himself'.

He could never have foreseen that, nearly a century later, Cocky would take his place in an exhibition tracing the military tradition of the Leith-Hay family.

Cocky would not have been surprised. He described himself as a warrior cockatoo. He was proud of his military career – a career, he said, that no other cockatoo had ever gone through.

Cocky's only regret – or perhaps the colonel's? – was that he never knew how old he was; no one, he said sadly, would ever know. The warrior cockatoo died at Leith Hall in 1908. He was buried with full military honours.

It is a long time since I first saw Cocky and I sometimes thought of him and wondered if something associated with him was on display at Leith Hall. I went back to Leith Hall and was shown the military section. Here were the Leith-Hay warriors, their uniforms, their weapons, their drums, their banners – I was walking through a great slice of north-east history.

But was Cocky, the cockatoo soldier, there? Well, on one display area I spotted a small book. On one of its corners were the initials 'CLH'. It was Cocky's book – and near it was a photograph of Cocky sitting on the shoulder of his master. Col. Alexander Sebastian Leith-Hay.

34

SLEEPYTOWN

I met in wi' Adam Mitchell,
Tae fee we did presume,
He's a fairmer in Kennethmont,
An he bides at Sleepytoon.

That verse from an old bothy ballad has always intrigued me. The name Sleepytoon conjures up a picture of a farm where the men spend half the day lazing among the hayricks, but it is clear from the ballad that Adam Mitchell would never have allowed that. He was the kind of farmer who boasted that his men never worked 'above ten hours a day'.

In my stravaiging about the north-east I have often come across a number of 'Sleepy' places and wondered how they got their names. For instance, the Sleepy Hillock is a landmark on an old drovers' road called the Ca', which runs from the Upper Don near Corgarff to Glen Gairn on Deeside. The word Ca' means a way for cattle out to the rough ground, but this track is barely visible now. Less than a mile to the west, beside *Carn Leac Saighdeir* [cairn of the soldier's grave], is the Laird's Bed, which was probably a hiding place and not simply somewhere to have a snooze.

The place-name expert William Alexander said that the name Sleepy Hillock occurred in various places in Scotland, often tied to legends about persons being put to sleep by fairies. In ghost-haunted Glen Ey there is a brae called *Cnoc chadail,* where a man was tempted into a hill by the fairies. When he came out seven years later he found that his bairns had grown up.

Alexander also mentioned Sleepy Hillocks at Corgarff and Huntly, a Sleepie Neuk at Forgue and a Sleepynook at Fyvie. The definition of a neuk is a recess, niche or crevice, so it is unlikely that any lairds sought shelter there. There was a Sleepy Hillock at Dyce on the fringe of Aberdeen airport. It went back to 1615, when it was spelt Sleipiehillock. It eventually changed to Mains of Kirkhill, but it was still known locally as 'Sleepies'. This Sleepy Hillock vanished when the airport was extended. There was also a Sleepy Knowe, a knoll south of Inchmarnoch.

It may be wrong to think of all these Sleepy Hillocks as places where people snatched forty winks, for another place-name expert, James Macdonald, rejected the whole idea. He was convinced that the old word was slippy or slippery, not sleepy. 'Slippy or slippery hillock', he said, came either from the steepness of the ground or from the fact that it was clay ground. He quoted weighty old tomes to prove his point: 1673, Slipie hillock, Court Books; 1645, Slipiehillock, Retour 281; 1614 Sleipihillock, Retour 131.

The only place I know that could call itself 'Sleepy' without argument is Sleepytoon, which lies a few miles from the village of Insch in the Garioch. Here, there was an ancient fair known as the Sleepy Market, and the reason that both it and the farm were dubbed 'Sleepy' was that the market began at sunset and ended one hour after sunrise next morning.

Sleepytown Farm was, and is, isolated from the rest of the community, tucked away in the lap of the Hill of Christ's Kirk, whose name once brought people to the area 'like bumbees buzzing frae a bike'. It is reached by a narrow road to the south-west of Insch. The track to the farm has a sign displaying the name 'Sleepytown'. There was once a piece of intricate woodcarving on it, showing an owl sitting on a tree with the moon shining out of a pitch-black sky and snow whitening the peak of a distant hill.

Here, when you hear the hoot of an owl it is a reminder that other nocturnal sounds were heard in this corner of the Garioch two centuries ago, for this was where the Sleepy Market was held. Its real name was Christ's Fair and by all accounts it was a riotous affair – 'a very singular market' was how Alford minister Rev. Gordon described it. It was turned into a daylight event about the middle of the eighteenth century, the reason being 'the excesses which had come to occur to it'.

It was said that the goings-on at the Sleepy Market became so scandalous that the local laird, General Hay of Rannes, ruled that it should become a daytime event. When it turned respectable it quickly lost its support and went out of existence, There is a less romantic theory that the Sleepy Market's name had nothing to do with the night-time roistering of the folk of Christ's Kirk, but that it originated in the Gaelic word *sliabh* or *sleibh* [hill] and that the market was held on top of the hill. The Hill of Christ's Kirk is a gentle, rounded hill (1,021 ft), scarcely a place where you expect to see 'all manner of wickedness' taking place.

I first saw this part of the north-east many years ago and thought it a remote and lonely place, full of strange-sounding names like the Dawache of Murriell and Seggiecrook, Edderlick and Old Flinders. There are actually three Flinders – Old Flinders, Little Flinders and New Flinders – all lying in the shadow of the Hill of Flinders. Tradition says that a colony of Flemings settled in Leslie and Kennethmont at a very early period and the name Flandres (sic) originated with them.

Then there is 'Christiskirk', mentioned in records going back to 'the yeir of God 1567'. The parish was once called Rathmoreal – the 'fort of Muir-gheal' – and the name is kept alive in the farm of Murrial, near Insch. At the farm of Christiskirk you find the last link with the original Christ's Kirk. In 1724 the Alford minister, Rev. Gordon, wrote of 'the ruins of a chappel, called Christ's Kirk and having a dyke encompassing it, where they are yet in use of burying their dead'.

When I went back to Sleepytown not long ago, I found that civilisation was creeping up on it. I drove up the road past Temple

The Hill of Christ's Kirk, scarcely a place where you expect to see 'all manner of wickedness'.

Croft, with the Hill of Christ's Kirk on my right, and I thought of all the scandalous affairs that were said to have taken place there. The hill, bright and colourful in the summer sunshine, held its secrets, and I came to a sign saying 'Sleepytown'. Across the road were the Christ's Kirk farm buildings. It was there that I met Vi and Alec Thomson, who had moved from Nairn to settle in this out-of-the-way corner. Alec had been with the police in London, in the Special Branch.

They had rented the farmhouse temporarily, for they were building their own house in a neighbouring field. Meantime, Christ's Kirk was choked with their furniture, leaving barely enough room to sleep. The farm was now owned by a London businessman, Nicholas Thomson, who also owned Sleepytown, which had been rented out to a couple, and the Flinders farms and other property. The Christ's Kirk farm buildings had all been converted into housing, including the steading, which had been turned into two houses.

We spoke about the time when there was a church in the vicinity, and I was told by the Thomsons that they had found a link with it only a step or two from their doorstep. There was a heap of rubble there, but Vi came upon a more definite find – a tombstone that had lain in the churchyard for four centuries.

The wood was thick and almost impenetrable and it was hard to visualise this wilderness as 'the toune and landis of Christiskirk and

The farm buildings at Christ's Kirk which have been converted to housing.

Temple Crofts'. But it took only a few minutes to push our way through grass and weeds to the tombstone. There had been other gravestones there, but there was no sign of them around us. Vi said some of the stones had been used to floor the steading. 'It's haunted now,' she said, jokingly, I think! The usual symbols were cut out on the stone, which lay flat on the ground. Father Time was there with his scythe – just in case he got it wrong there was a timer beside him – and at the foot of the stone there was a skull in which two large holes had been cut out where the sockets would have been. They had given Vi the fright of her life when she cleaned the stone. 'It was quite

Vi Thomson at the ancient tombstone she found in the wood hear her house.

creepy,' she said. 'I scrubbed it, then I poured water on it. The water filled the holes in the skull and suddenly it was all light and two eyes staring at me. I thought, "Oh, I'd better get out of here."'

Vi read the writing on the stone, or as much as she could, for some of it had worn away. This was what it said, 'Here lies James Leggan sometime farmer at Upper Eden Garioch, died November —— 1657 aged 47 years. Lauful husband to Kethiren Milne —— at the care of her late spouse —— .'

So out of that wood came a little bit of history. Vi pointed out the heap of rubble where it was said the church had been. She was told it had been a wooden kirk. Who James Leggan was I will never know, only that he was a farmer and that he died at a comparatively early age. There is, or was, a farm called Edengarioch near Premnay, only a few miles away. He probably worshipped at Christ's Kirk.

I left Christ's Kirk, wishing the Thomsons well, giving a parting nod to Sleepytoon and a knowing wink to the Hill of Christ's Kirk, still wondering about those 'excesses' which made General Hay of Rannes take the sleep out of Sleepy Market. The general was a hardened soldier and it must have taken a good deal to make him take such a step.

In the middle of the nineteenth century Adam Mitchell, who featured in the Sleepytoon bothy ballad, had five servants running the farm. One of them, William Clark, didn't think much of the way the men were treated. When he had been fee'd there Mitchell promised better things. 'If you and I agree,' he said, 'Ye'll hae the fairest play, fir I never bid my servants work above ten hours a day.'

The farmer put Clark on to laying turnips down when he started work and later he was sent with another man, Knowles, to 'ca' the dung'. The rain came on and they were told to lowse [stop work]. It began to come down in torrents and Adam Mitchell said it was time to fill their bellies, but how he filled their bellies sparked off revolt among the men.

The rain it soon went over,
And the day began to break,
And oor neist orders wis tae scrape
Oor denners fae the secks [sacks]

We'll ne'er refuse what you command,
What e'er ye bid us do,
But tae eat the scrapins o the secks
Is a thing we'll never do.

Oh ye daur refuse your order,
Oh the scoundrels that ye are,
But ye bargained for ten hours a day,
Refuse them if ye daur.

The orders wis tae bed at nine,
And never leave the toun,
And for every time ye left it
We wis fined half-a-croon.

Knowles wis fined mony a time
But never lost the hert,
And I masel wis fined a poun
For turnin up a cairt.

The Martinmas term came round and the men left Sleepytown –
'We'll awa tae Rhynie Fair and there we'll hae some fun.' Clark swore
to tell the world of 'aa the usage that we had at Sleepytoon'. The bothy
ballad ended like this,

I still see Auld Adam yet,
Suppin his dish o brose,
I think I'll send him a hankie
Just tae dicht his stuffy nose.

William Alexander, in his *Bards of Bon-Accord* (1887), wrote about 'the
kind of popular song that prevailed upwards of a century ago'. He said
that many of them were 'too broad and coarse for reproduction at this
time of day'. They contained dirt, but it was all on the surface. He
quoted a song called 'The Sleepy Merchant', where the merchant lay
in his bed and his lady gave him a dram and 'bade him drink and lie
down'. It ended with the merchant marrying her, 'He's tane the lassie
by the hand, And tied her up in bedlock band, And now she is the

merchant's wife, And she lives in Aberdeen.'

What Adam Mitchell would have said about it is anybody's guess. He might have given a sniff and told the merchant to see that she worked her ten hours a day.

35

THE SOLDIER STONE

They called it the 'Soldier Stone'. I saw it when I was driving through the Avon valley on Speyside, near the Brig of A'an. It stood on a grassy ledge where the ground sloped down to the River Avon, and the only inscription on it was the date – 1690. That was the year in which the Battle of Cromdale was fought.

The stone marked the burial place of a Highland soldier who died of wounds received at the battle. It was only about two feet high, yet it had more poignancy than any towering monument to the war dead, for it stood over the grave of an Unknown Soldier of nearly four centuries ago.

The battle was fought in the Haughs of Cromdale – the 'crooked plain' they called it – set against the hills of Cromdale. This backdrop formed a ridge that stretched for some eight miles between the Spey and the Avon. I remember tramping across those flat, peaty heights

The Soldier Stone on the B9136 road from Bridge of Avon. It marks the burial place of a Highland soldier who died of wounds in the Battle of Cromdale.

some years ago, looking for some sign of the struggle whose outcome was recorded in an old song, telling how the Highland army rued 'that e'er they came to Cromdale'. Its final lines were 'But, alas, we could no longer stay, Sae owre the hills we came away; And sore do we lament the day that e'er we came to Cromdale.'

Up on those windy hills I could see where the two armies met under the shadow of Craigan a' Chaise (2,367 ft), the highest point in the Cromdales, where there is a cairn commemorating Queen Victoria's golden jubilee in 1887. Below, spreading out from Claggersnich Wood, was the bleak moorland where the English horses 'bathed their hoofs in Highland blood'.

It all began when an army of rebellious Jacobites marched through Strathspey, plundering and burning as it went. On the night of 30 April 1690 they set up camp in the Haughs of Cromdale, around the ruined Castle of Lethendry. Their leader, Col. Cannon, had a force of 1,500, made up of MacDonald, MacLean, Cameron and MacPherson clansmen, along with the Grants of Invermoriston. Sir Thomas Livingstone, commander of the royal forces, who was stationed in Inverness, hurried south on hearing of the Jacobites' movements. He had with him the local Grants of Strathspey, six troops of Scots Dragoons, a battalion of foot soldiers and two troops of cavalry.

On the evening before the battle, Cannon's men were camped at Lethendry, a farm close to Cromdale, unaware that the government troops had come down to the Spey from the Dava Moor. At dawn on 1 May, Jacobite troops were spotted crossing the Spey and the alarm was raised. Sir Thomas decided to mount a sudden attack on the Jacobite camp. A Crown Estate plaque above the Soldier Stone tells what happened.

Part of the way was concealed by birch and the attack was so sudden that many of the clansmen had no time to reach for their belted plaids or weapons. Those who faced the enemy could give only faint resistance. About 400 were killed or captured on the day with officers rounded up in Lethendry castle and mill. Some Camerons and MacLeans were pursued across the Spey and caught and killed near Aviemore and short of the safety of the crags of Craigellachie.

According to General Mackay, army commander in Scotland at

the time, the government's forces lost no soldiers and only eight horses, their success being due to three factors: (1) locked gates at Castle Grant, Grantown-on-Spey prevented anyone leaving to warn the Jacobite force; (2) the cavalry approached through a narrow pass (presumably by Huntly's Cave) and were not ambushed; (3) the Jacobite forces were not camped on the usual defendable, broken ground but on open ground.

'It was more of a routing than a battle,' it said on the plaque. I was thinking of that as I stood by the Soldier Stone. When Cannon made that dawn attack on the Jacobite camp, those who faced

The Soldier Stone.

them could give only faint resistance. Many were captured in the Haughs, others were rounded up in Lethendry castle and mill. When panic set in, many men fled naked, some up the northern slopes of the Cromdales (which were too steep for the horses), and descended to Avonside. The plaque on the fence tells of one man who, badly wounded, died from his wounds above the Avon. There was nothing to show who he was, or where he came from. It was more than likely that in some Highland home a family would have mourned him, not knowing where he was, or even that he had been decently buried.

When I came down from the hills on that visit to the Cromdales, I passed the *Clach nam Piobait* [the Piper's Stone], where a Jacobite piper is said to have made his last stand. There was an unimpressive memorial there, a plain stone wedged against a tree on the edge of Claggersnich Wood. I remember writing then that the folk of Cromdale should erect another cairn on top of the hill to commemorate the battle.

Meantime, that simple stone above the Avon, with its date 1690, will be a reminder to people passing that way that this was where one victim of that bloody encounter was buried in a lonely grave.

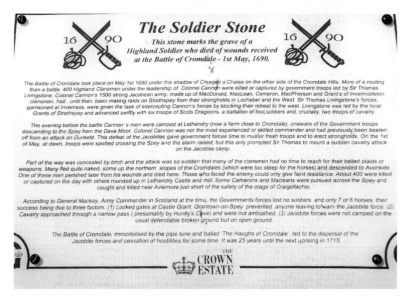

This plaque tells the story of the Soldier Stone.

189

36

THE FINTRAY PRESS

The village of Hatton of Fintray hides away from the world about a mile north of Kinaldie, which was once a station on the now-disused main line of the Great North of Scotland Railway (GNSR). The railway was built on the bed of the Aberdeenshire Canal, whose flyboats plied between Port Elphinstone and Aberdeen. When the canal was opened in 1806, a gun boomed out as the first barge set off on its historic journey, but less than half a century later the dream dried up when the canal was drained to make way for the GNSR. Now the railway has gone.

Ten minutes' walk from Kinaldie is a bridge that spans the River Don at the Boat of Hatton, where a ferry once operated. Hatton of Fintray lies ahead. It is a tree-girt little community, which at one time had three annual fairs, but over the years Fintray has shrunk into itself. There is little now that holds it to the past, except, perhaps, the parish church – a great, gaunt building standing high on a knoll at the north end of the village. It was from this quiet backwater 200 years ago that a chapbook was launched that became a phenomenal success. Its title page carried these lines, 'O mother dear, make me my bed, And lay my face to Fyvie; Thus will I lie, and thus will die, For my dear Andrew Lammie.'

This was a verse from a ballad called *Mill of Tifty's Annie*, a sweet, sad tale of a lass who loved the trumpeter of Fyvie, but whose parents tried to break up the relationship. Annie was a real person – Agnes Smith, daughter of the miller of Tifty, who violently opposed the affair. It was a doomed romance, for Annie was beaten by her family for her attraction to Andrew Lammie – 'her brother strike her wondrous sore' – and in the end the lovers were parted. It was said that Annie died of a broken heart as well as a broken body.

Mill of Tifty's Annie was the first chapbook issued from the Fintray Press. Thousands of copies were sold up and down the haughs of Aberdeenshire, along with other popular ballads put out by this fledgling chapbook publisher. Nobody knew who he was, and nobody knew how the Fintray Press had come to put its roots down in the back-of-beyond at Hatton of Fintray.

'Few people outside these valleys have ever heard of the Fintray Press,' wrote Aberdeen's city librarian, George M. Fraser, in his book *The Lone Shieling,* published in 1908. 'In the city of Aberdeen itself, within a dozen miles of where the Press operates, not every hundreth person can tell you where it is carried on, and not one in a thousand could tell what kind of literature Fintray Press supplies.' Fraser said that Hatton of Fintray was a very secluded hamlet when *Mill of Tifty's Annie* was first printed, adding that it was 'just about as secluded still, although it lies within a mile of the Great North of Scotland Railway'.

When I set off for Hatton of Fintray to see where *Mill of Tifty's Annie* had its birth pains. I wondered if one in every hundredth person would know today about the Fintray Press and who ran it, or, for that matter, how many people knew anything about Fintray itself. Fraser described how he got to it.

> You take a slow train from Aberdeen [he wrote], for fast trains fly contemptuously past the stations in that neighbourhood, and in half an hour you alight at Kinaldie (pronounced Kin-a-die), whence a brisk ten minutes' walk carries you by an iron girder bridge over the Don, and so to the compact little village of Hatton of Fintray.

There were no fast trains flying contemptuously past when I was there, and no flyboats chugging up the Aberdeenshire Canal. It was a pity for it seemed to me that a flyboat would have been the right sort of transport in which to approach sleepy Fintray. I was looking for a little merchant's shop, or the remains of it, or even some idea of where it had been, for that was where it all began. The old smiddy stands on the road through Fintray, but now it is a garage. Two or three doors down there was a small post office, and the 'shoppie' may have been there, but no one knew.

The shop was run by a Mrs Cumming, whose son John helped her. Eventually it was decided that John should go to Aberdeen to learn how business was carried on in the big city. So off he went to Kinaldie and boarded a flyboat on the Aberdeenshire Canal. There were no guns booming when young Cumming sailed away to carve out a future for himself, but in Aberdeen he learned more than how to handle the small wares of a country merchant. When he came back to Fintray to help his mother in the shop his ideas had radically changed.

He had become interested in printing, and particularly the printing of ballad literature. He knew William Thom, the 'Inverury poet', who lived at no great distance from Fintray, and in Aberdeen he had come to know John Longmuir, editor of the abridged edition of Jamieson's *Scottish Dictionary*, author of a highly praised guide to Dunnottar, and a score of other works.

Longmuir, who later became an LLD, encouraged him to try his hand at printing chapbooks and suggested possible woodcuts for the 'chaps' – the rig of a vessel (Longmuir was minister of the Sailors' Church in Aberdeen), the 'make' of a Highlandman's bagpipes or the architecture of the Auld Kirk o' Pert, which ornamented the cover of *The Herd's Ghaist*. He cut out the blocks for the woodcuts himself.

He had a printing press built into one end of his shop and it was there that his first chapbook was produced: *The Old Scottish Ballad of Andrew Lammie* or *Mill of Tifty's Annie*. It was said to be the best-known ballad in all the Howe of Buchan. It consisted of a sheet of eight pages. 'Chapman billies' sold it for a halfpenny at farm kitchen doors and dealers bought it for three-halfpence per dozen. It was a resounding success, a nineteenth-century bestseller.

George Fraser printed a list of the chapbooks published by the Fintray Press. The total ran to twenty-one eight-page chapbooks. 'Each one,' he wrote, 'had been reprinted over and over again, although the demand for them fell away when the daily newspaper began to absorb the spare time of the peasantry, as of greater people.' The list included such intriguing titles as *The Blue Peat Reek*, *The Love of Barley Bree*, *Grigor's Ghost* (an old Scotch song), *The Water Warbler*, containing the Cogie, *The Covenanter's Carousal* and *Fa Pushioned the Doggies*.

But nothing could outdo the *Mill of Tifty's Annie*, which headed the list. It sold well over 100,000 copies, yet the printer's profits on the ballad were small. Today, you would be hard put to find any of them, least of all *Tifty's Annie*. If you did it would be a great curiosity, an antiquarian treasure. There are no more chapbooks on Tifty's Annie, and down in Fintray there is nothing to remind you of her – or of John Cumming, the local lad who told her story and put this little village on the publishing map.

37

LAIRD ON A FOOTPLATE

Up on the Muir of Dinnet, where the Deeside railway track, now a walkway, runs from Dinnet to Ballater, a curious wooden gate stands near the line. It is called a half-gate. It seemed to me to be a gate to nowhere, so I decided to find out who built it, and why. To get the full story I had to go back to the late nineteenth century, when railway fever gripped the country.

There were a number of paths weaving their way through Dinnet estate at one time, mostly used by staff on their bikes. One was called the Keeper's path, while another had a name suggesting a higher social scale – the Butler's roadie. They had twenty living-in staff in Dinnet House, but those days have gone and most of the paths with them.

One path led from Dinnet House to the half-gate. It was laid out for the laird, Sir (Charles) Malcolm Barclay-Harvey. It was an unofficial 'stop' on the Deeside line. Farther up the line was Cambus o' May,

The author at the half-gate on the Deeside line.

a small, single-platform station picturesquely situated beside the River Dee. Opened in 1876, it was designated a 'halt', but there were no platforms or paying passengers at the half-gate. It was for the laird's personal use. He knew the drivers and firemen on the Deeside line. He would come down through the moor by the path from Dinnet House, climb up on to the footplate and ride into Ballater with the crew.

The half-gate was to him what the looking-glass was to Alice in *Alice in Wonderland*, for when he went through it he entered another world – an exciting world of steam and speed. The locomotives that passed up the Deeside line deafened the ears and dazzled the eyes. Their engines were painted dark blue with black lines and, as Sir Malcolm wrote, 'always kept in magnificent condition'. One engine was painted tartan, either Royal Stuart or Duff, some had copper chimney caps and painted domes, and two had 'stovepipe' chimneys and large polished brass domes.

I first heard about Sir Malcolm and the half-gate from my father-in-law, Bill Rae, who was a driver on the Deeside line. Other stories about him drifted down through the years. 'He was an interesting man,' said Bill Gillanders, head forester on the Dinnet estate who sadly died early in 2005. I was put in touch with Bill by the present laird, Marcus Humphrey, Sir Malcolm's grandson, but by a curious coincidence I already knew him. He once took me on a Land Rover tour of the Morven heights when I was writing about that area. He confirmed that Barclay-Harvey had ridden on the Deeside trains. He mentioned a driver called Lamb, who often took him on the footplate.

The name struck a chord with me. 'Was his first name Sandy?' I asked. Bill said it was, so here was another coincidence for I had known Sandy Lamb before the war. My father-in-law and Sandy were friends, working on the same railway line. Sandy owned property in Aberdeen and when my wife and I were house-hunting after the war we rented our first home from him.

Sir Malcolm had a passion for railways that stayed with him all his life. Marcus Humphrey recalled how in 1947, when he was a boy, his grandfather took him across the moor from Dinnet House to see the king's train come up the line. He shared his interest with another laird, Sir Ian Forbes-Leith of Fyvie. They both went to meetings of the Great North of Scotland Railway Association.

But Sir Malcolm's enthusiasm for trains went far beyond Deeside. From 1939 to 1944 he was governor of South Australia and during the time he took a great interest in Australian railway affairs. He admired the railways 'down under' and on 5 November 1943, a new streamline train was named after him. For two days, locomotive 520 'Sir Malcolm Barclay-Harvey' was put on display at Adelaide station before beginning its working life. Today, more than sixty years later, No.520 is still chugging through the hill country in Australia.

It was on Deeside that I went in search of the half-gate. It may have been the time of the year, or the weather, but the Muir of Dinnet had a desolate look about it. The track without its rails looked barren and forgotten. I would have been happy if I had heard the hoot of a train coming up behind me. Across the moor I could see the flagpole on the tower at Dinnet House. Not far beyond this point I came to the mysterious half-gate.

I had expected to see a broken, ruinous gate, or a conventional gate with half of it lying in the heather. Instead I found two half-gates, one on either side of the track. The two gates allowed visitors to Dinnet House to cross the track and follow a path to one of the lodges, while the first gate was also the 'stop' for Sir Malcolm's visits to the footplate.

What caught my eye were two heavy metal posts on either side of the gate, railway posts, similar to others that I had seen on the way up.

Dinnet House in the woods near the old Deeside track.

They seemed to point to the fact that the gate had been built not by the estate but by the Great North of Scotland Railway. In other words, the company not only turned a blind eye to the laird riding on their engines but also thought it in their best interests to build a gate as an unofficial 'halt' for him.

The half-gate allowed only one person through at a time. When I was pinned in the middle of it, I suddenly realised that it was really a version of the old-style kissing gate – a leftover from a more romantic age.

The station at Dinnet is no great distance from the half-gate. The railway may have gone, but a sign on the wall of the station buildings still tells the world that this is 'DINNET'. Oddly enough, the spelling Dinnatie was common until about 1800. The name Dinnet originally belonged to the boat and mill of Dinnet at the east end of the moor.

Whatever the name, there is virtually nothing to show that it was once a busy station. Walkers heading up the track from the station pass a deep passage cut out of the ground, with heavy stone walls on either side. This was once a siding, now it is choked with trees that have grown to full height. The same thing has happened opposite

The railway buildings at Dinnet, now used as estate offices.

the station buildings, where a virtual woodland has sprouted in the track itself.

The signal-box has gone, which is a shame, for I imagine it might have been turned into a tourist attraction. George Watson, a veteran railwayman who served in all the Deeside stations except Dess, was in charge of the signal-box when the tsar of Russia passed through the station in 1896 on his way to Balmoral. His train consisted of sixteen carriages carrying ten tons of luggage.

The Victorian station building is still there, but ironically it shows its back to the main road. You have to go on to the old platform to appreciate it. It was probably the most interesting railway building on the Deeside line. In 1957, *The Railway Magazine* carried a piece about Dinnet station and mentioned the buildings. This is what it said,

> The bleakness of the heather-clad moor is emphasised by the fences which protect exposed sections of the railway from winter snowdrifts. The buildings on the eastbound platform of Dinnet are unlike those at other stations on the line, and appear to have remained unaltered since they were built for the Aboyne & Braemar Company ninety years ago (1867).

The Dinnet estate no doubt makes good use of the old station building, but it is a pity that its quaint Victorian style is hidden from the public eye. It would be well worthwhile turning it into a visitor centre where, through exhibits and pictures, the story of the Deeside line could be told. Tourists could learn about Queen Victoria and other royal travellers using the line, about foreign guests like the tsar and tsarina of Russia, and about the half-gate, which was the laird of Dinnet's private doorway to the magical world of railways.

Note: Nearly forty years have passed since the last passenger train ran between Aberdeen and Ballater, but there are still railway coaches on the Deeside line. The Royal Deeside Railway Preservation Society have two coaches at Milton of Crathes, where visitors can take a peep into the past – and dream about the return of the trains in the future.